LATIMER PUBLICATIONS

From Cambridge to Colony

Charles Simeon's Enduring Influence on Christianity in Australia

EDWARD LOANE (EDITOR)

The Latimer Trust

From Cambridge to Colony: Charles Simeon's Enduring Influence on Christianity in Australia © The Latimer Trust 2016

ISBN 978-1-906327-38-5

Cover photo: Charles Simeon's teapot and preaching Bible © Margaret Hobbs. Reverse cover: Memorial to Charles Simeon in Holy Trinity Church, Cambridge © Margaret Hobbs

Published by the Latimer Trust February 2016

The Latimer Trust
London N14 4PS UK
Registered Charity: 1084337
Company Number: 4104465
Web: www.latimertrust.org
E-mail: administrator@latimertrust.org

CONTENTS

Contributors 1

Preface – *Mark Thompson* 3

1. Introduction – *Edward Loane* 5

2. The Cambridge Connection: Charles Simeon, Australia and the
Cambridge Evangelicals – *Craig Schwarze* 11
2.1.   *The English Evangelical Revival* 11
2.2.   *Henry Venn* 13
2.3.   *The Universities* 14
2.4.   *The Magdalene Evangelicals* 16
2.5.   *William Farish* 16
2.6.   *The Elland Clerical Society* 18
2.7.   *Hull Grammar School* 19
2.8.   *Isaac Milner* 20
2.9.   *Charles Simeon* 21
2.10.   *The Cambridge Evangelicals and Australia* 23

3. Charles Simeon's Influence on Samuel Marsden's Chaplaincy in
New South Wales – *David Pettett* 25
3.1.   *Simeon's Influence – Preaching* 26
3.2.   *Simeon's Influence – Magistracy* 33
3.3.   *Simeon's Influence – Mission* 35
3.4.   *Conclusions* 37

4. Shaping the Anglican Church in Sydney, 1855-1882: Charles
Simeon's Influence on Frederic Barker – *Grant Maple* 39
4.1.   *Charles Simeon's Direct Influence at Cambridge, 1827-1830* 40
4.2.   *Charles Simeon's Indirect Influence through Fellow Evangelicals* ...45
4.3.   *Frederic Barker's Parish Ministry: Upton, Ireland, Edge Hill and
        Baslow* 47
4.4.   *Barker's Leadership of Sydney Diocese* 51
4.5.   *Barker's Enduring Influence on the Character of the Diocese.* 55

5. From King's College to Kingsford: Charles Simeon's Enduring
Influence on Australian University Ministry – *Edward Loane* 57
5.1.   *Simeon's University Ministry* 59
5.2.   *What Sprang From Simeon's Ministry?* 63
5.3.   *Phillip Jensen's Ministry at UNSW* 65
5.4.   *Conclusion* 68

6. Moderate Biblicism: How Charles Simeon's Theology Shaped His Relationship to the Church of England, Non-Conformists, and the Dissenter Movements – *James Snare*.................................69

6.1.   *Simeon's Approach to Theological Differences*........................... 69
6.2.   *Simeon's Moderate Approach in Relationship to Others*...............77
6.3.   *An Evaluation of Simeon's Approach*.....................................82

7. 'Loving in Deed and in Truth': The Practical Evangelicalism of Charles Simeon (1759-1836) – *David Furse-Roberts*.......................... 85

7.1.   *Simeon's Activist Evangelicalism*...85
7.2.   *Simeon's Legacy for Australia* 88
7.3.   *Conclusion* 91

8. Bibliography...92

8.1.   *Primary Sources* 92
8.2.   *Secondary Sources* 92

Contributors

David Furse-Roberts holds a PhD from the University of New South Wales where he wrote a thesis on the British social reformer, Lord Shaftesbury (1801-1885), and the evolving character of Victorian Evangelicalism. His thesis explored how the tradition of Anglican Evangelicalism contributed to the life and work of this eminent Victorian statesman. Current research interests include Evangelical church history together with broader religious and political movements of the nineteenth and twentieth centuries.

Edward Loane has been a lecturer in Doctrine and Church History at Moore College since 2014. He completed his BD at Moore College in 2007 and served in parish ministry in Sydney's south west until he began his doctorate at Cambridge in October 2011. Edward's research interests include the history of Anglicanism in Australia and England.

Grant Maple has recently retired as Academic Dean, School of Christian Studies, Robert Menzies College, Macquarie University. He was the Editor of the *Journal of Christian Education* before it amalgamated in 2015 to become the *International Journal of Christianity and Education*. On top of his BA and BD, Grant has completed an MA and PhD in the discipline of Australian church history.

David Pettett is currently undertaking doctoral studies at Macquarie University examining the sermons of Samuel Marsden. David is an Anglican minister in Sydney and he has special responsibility for the Diocesan Chaplains in prisons and hospitals. David has been a hospital chaplain and a prison chaplain as well as a chaplain in the Royal Australian Navy. He has held various parish positions in Sydney Diocese and has been a missionary, church planting in Japan. David was an editor for a previous publication of Moore College Library Day papers, *Launching Marsden's Mission: The Beginnings of the Church Missionary Society in New Zealand, viewed from New South Wales*.

Craig Schwarze is an independent researcher who has previously given several papers on religion in early Colonial Australia. He is currently finalising a new biography of Richard Johnson, with publication expected in late 2016.

James Snare has a Bachelor of Arts in History and English Literature from The University of Melbourne and has just completed his Bachelor of Divinity from Moore College. In 2016 James will serve an Assistant Minister at Gosford Presbyterian Church and hopes to pursue further research in historical or philosophical theology in the near future.

Preface – *Mark Thompson*

One of my favourite images of church history is that of the family photo album. Perhaps it is not as popular as in the past, given the advent of digital photography and the possibility of taking and storing hundreds of images of a single event. Yet in many families taking out the family album and looking through old photographs of people and events long gone is an important activity in building and maintaining family identity. Remember when this happened? Remember her? We are shaped by the people and events of the past much more than we ever admit. It is like that with the family history of the people of God. It is important regularly to get out the family album, dust it off, and remember who we are and what has shaped us to be the people we are today.

Charles Simeon is certainly one of those whose influence continues to be felt in the Church of England and in evangelicalism worldwide. Undoubtedly quirky in manner, but resolute in his commitment to the gospel of Christ and the mission of taking that gospel to all of England and throughout the world, Simeon directly influenced three generations of gospel workers, not least by the way he endured considerable opposition as he sought to take the gospel to his beloved Cambridge. The story of his tenure of Holy Trinity Cambridge is a study in faithfulness but also of Christian patience and fortitude. His God-given capacity to inspire men to give themselves to the proclamation of Christ and the salvation he has won for us, no matter how difficult the surrounding circumstances may be, was truly remarkable and continues to bear fruit. Even in Australia, on the other side of the world and two hundred years on, an incalculable debt is owed under God to this man, by those who have no idea at all who he was.

The essays in this little volume are a welcome addition to the steadily growing study of Simeon, his faith, his methods and his influence. That they should emerge from a conference in a small evangelical Anglican theological college on the other side of the world from Simeon's most direct arena of activity is a further testimony to his influence. If they stimulate further perusal of the evangelical family album all the better.

Back in 1996 I borrowed from the Bodleian Library in Oxford the first volume of Simeon's magnum opus, his *Horae Homileticae*. It famously contains the three questions by which Simeon hoped all his preaching would be judged: 'Does it uniformly tend to humble the sinner? To exalt the Saviour? To promote holiness?' The Bodleian copy also contains this inscription: 'To the Chancellor and Scholars at Oxford for the Bodleian Library. A present from the Author in the humble hope, and with earnest prayer to God, that his efforts to diffuse the knowledge of Christ with all the wonders of Redeeming Love may not be in vain. Ch. Simeon, King's College Cambridge 1833'. In the essays which follow you will find ample evidence to conclude that his hope was realised and his prayers answered with a resounding 'yes'.

1. Introduction – *Edward Loane*

Towards the back of the majestic – some Australians may say ostentatious – chapel of King's College, Cambridge, a plain and simple tile is inscribed with two letters and four numbers: C.S. 1836. This humble memorial is a testament to the character of Charles Simeon, a servant of Christ who exercised an extraordinary influence on the shape and expansion of Evangelical Christianity. The significant impact of Simeon's ministry was evident in his own lifetime, but its enduring and expansive legacy would have been impossible to imagine. This volume is a small contribution to the understanding of Simeon's influence, particularly focusing on how he shaped, and still shapes, Evangelical Christianity in Australia.

It is fitting that there is a memorial to Simeon in the chapel at King's. It was in that place, at the Easter Day Holy Communion service in 1779, that he experienced for the first time the liberating power of forgiveness that had been won for him in the death of Christ. He recalled, 'From that hour peace flowed in rich abundance into my soul; and at the Lord's Table in our chapel I had the sweetest access to God through my blessed Saviour.'[1] Although his childhood had been marked by wealth and privilege, Simeon had come to realise his spiritual poverty and absolute helplessness without Christ and, as such, he entrusted himself to God's grace. In doing so he received an imperishable treasure of infinite magnitude. Simeon invested the rest of his life in propagating this life-giving gospel.

Simeon never left the shores of Great Britain. With the exception of a couple of preaching tours to Scotland, he rarely left the south east of England and the vast majority of his time was spent in a small town in East Anglia. It was a strategic town, however, with the colleges of the ancient university bringing the potential crème of society into close living quarters. Simeon's global impact was exercised through his influence on young men who came to study at Cambridge and then went on to be leaders in England and abroad.

---

[1] William Carus, *Memoirs of the Life of the Revd Charles Simeon*, 3rd edn (London: Hatchard and Son, 1847), p 9.

It was in this fashion that Simeon came to be so influential on Christianity in Australia. The first two chaplains to the new colony were his protégés. These men were effective in setting the tone for Christianity in Sydney: enterprising Evangelical endeavour. Moreover, the longest serving bishop of Sydney Diocese was also personally shaped by Simeon. The ministries of these three men are highlighted in this volume. Simeon's legacy in Australia, however, is greater than just the men he personally influenced. The latter chapters of this volume demonstrate other ways he has been significant, whether through the model of ministry he exercised, or the tone in which it was conducted.

There are, of course, numerous other people and ministries that could have been included in our study. Perhaps most notably, this volume lacks a specific treatment of Simeon's influence on Charles Perry, and the way that shaped his ministry as the first Bishop of Melbourne (1847-1876). Perry had been a sceptical undergraduate of Trinity College who eventually began attending Simeon's services in a clandestine manner. He was converted and went on to serve in a Cambridge parish and planted another church. Eleven years after Simeon's death, Perry was consecrated and left England for a diocese on the other side of the world which at that time comprised of three clergy and one church building.[2] The discovery of gold just a few years later brought spectacular growth to Perry's diocese which he managed to shape into a bastion of Evangelical Anglicanism. More work could be done investigating Simeon's influence on Perry and Melbourne Diocese. A more detailed study of Simeon's relative impact in Sydney through Bishop Barker compared with his impact in Melbourne through Bishop Perry would also be rewarding. These remain as projects for another time.

The chapters that are presented in this volume were each papers delivered at the 2015 Moore College Library Day. The Library Day is a public conference held at Moore College which is generally focused on Australian church history. It also aims to display some of the many treasures held in the Moore College Library. The 2015 conference included displays of numerous nineteenth century works by and about Charles Simeon, as well as several personal letters written by Simeon himself. These letters were generously loaned to the college for the day by Simon Manchester who has a substantial collection of early

---

[2] Hugh Evans Hopkins, *Charles Simeon of Cambridge* (Eugene, Oregon: Wipf & Stock, 1977), p 115.

Evangelical memorabilia. Manchester has exercised a long and fruitful ministry at St Thomas', North Sydney, and in an interview he shared with the conference how Simeon had been personally influential on him. This reinforced the enduring nature of Simeon's impact. Unfortunately it was not possible to include an account of this interview in this book.

Within this volume, Craig Schwarze's chapter explores what he has called 'the Cambridge connection'. He surveys a number of key Evangelical personalities and organisations that both pre-dated Simeon and supported his ministry in Cambridge. Schwarze goes on to show how these networks functioned in nurturing and promoting young men for Christian ministry and how the first three chaplains appointed to the Colony in New South Wales were all products of this recruiting and training scheme that brought them into contact with Simeon in Cambridge.

In the next chapter, David Pettett focuses on how influential Simeon was on the second chaplain to arrive in Australia, Samuel Marsden. In a detailed study of the primary sources Pettett demonstrates how heavily Marsden relied on Simeon's sermon outlines when preparing his own sermons. He goes on to show that Marsden's understanding of the role of the Magistracy and Mission were both consistent with Simeon's beliefs, which serves as further evidence for Simeon's impact on Australia (and New Zealand) through one of his most devoted disciples.

Grant Maple's chapter is devoted to an evaluation of Simeon's influence on Frederic Barker, the second Bishop of Sydney. Barker's episcopate was arguably the most significant in establishing the theological character of Sydney Diocese. He was responsible for establishing many of the Diocese's most important institutions such as its Synod and Moore College. Maple shows the way Simeon directly guided Barker as an undergraduate and also how Simeon indirectly shaped him through the ministry of John Bird Sumner.[3] In each case, the numerous influences of Simeon are demonstrated in the way Barker exercised his ministry.

---

[3] Sumner was Simeon's 'most preferred' student, rising to become Archbishop of Canterbury. In the King's College dining hall Simeon's portrait and Sumner's portrait hang on opposite sides facing each other. It causes one to ponder what they may have talked about together (was it their plans to promote Evangelical Christianity?) while they ate meals in that same hall.

Chapter five establishes the enduring impact that Simeon has had on Christianity in Australia by concentrating on student ministry. It looks at the pioneering efforts of Simeon in ministering to university students and traces this development through to the International Fellowship of Evangelical Students. The chapter shows how Evangelical students at Australian universities cherish standing in the Simeon tradition and goes on to demonstrate the direct impact that reading about Charles Simeon had on Phillip Jensen's hugely significant ministry to students at The University of New South Wales.

James Snare's chapter is a contribution to the scholarly debate surrounding Simeon's approach to theologically divisive issues. Snare discusses Simeon's methodological approach to his theology and his biblical priority. He then illustrates how this theology was applied in a variety of relationships and offers critical evaluation of Simeon's stance. While this chapter does not directly deal with any events in Australia, it is a very helpful analysis of an Evangelical method that is still commonly employed by Christians in Australia, particularly those who identify themselves as standing in the Simeon tradition.

This volume concludes with David Furse-Roberts' chapter exploring Simeon's social action. Some historians have been critical of Simeon's apparent lack of social engagement. For example, Roger Steer claims that 'Unlike other Evangelicals [Simeon] did not espouse the cause of the abolition of the slave trade; nor indeed that of any other social reform.'[4] Furse-Roberts' work demonstrates how Simeon did, indeed, exhibit the 'activist' trait that David Bebbington included in his popular definition of Evangelicalism.[5] Furthermore, Furse-Roberts goes on to survey three prominent Sydney clergymen who followed in this aspect of the Simeon tradition.

Charles Simeon's ministry has had, and continues to have, a truly global impact. This volume begins to demonstrate how that influence has been played out on the other side of the world in Australia. Although Simeon's education, social standing and disposition inclined him towards being proud, he worked hard to display the fruit of humility. John Thornton may have had this tendency in mind when he encouraged Simeon that the three lessons a minister had to learn were:

---

4 Roger Steer, *Church on Fire: The Story of Anglican Evangelicals* (London: Hodder & Stoughton, 1998), p 167.

5 David Bebbington, *Evangelicalism in Modern Britain: A History from the 1730s to the 1980s* (London: Unwin Hyman, 1989), p 3.

'I. *Humility.* – 2. *Humility.* – 3. *Humility.*'[6] The small, plain tile at the back of King's College chapel is a testimony to the fact that Simeon had learnt this lesson. That tile is a small tribute to Simeon and this volume is offered as a similar tribute. It must be remembered, however, that Simeon was merely a servant that the Lord Almighty used in powerful ways and all his efforts were directed towards magnifying his saviour Jesus Christ. *Soli Deo Gloria.*

---

6   Handley Carr Glyn Moule, *Charles Simeon* (London: Methuen & Co., 1892), p 81.

2. The Cambridge Connection: Charles Simeon, Australia and the Cambridge Evangelicals – *Craig Schwarze*

One of the events of historical note in Australia recently was the death of former Prime Minister Gough Whitlam.[1] Regardless of one's politics, he must be acknowledged as a remarkable man. His legend grew to enormous proportions, even within his own lifetime. As Malcolm Turnbull affectionately noted, it got to the point where he was often given credit for things he had not actually done. Indeed, I was very interested to learn from an ABC *vox pop* that Whitlam was responsible for giving the vote to Australian women – and not before time, let me add.[2]

This book focuses on another remarkable man, one who also had a profound impact on Australian history – although somewhat indirectly. That man is Charles Simeon. But, like Whitlam, although it is right for us to acknowledge the significant impact of Simeon, in some cases I fear that he is given more credit than he might rightly claim. This is particularly the case in the common idea that Simeon was virtually solely responsible for the Evangelical awakening that occurred in Cambridge during the 1780s.

In fact, a small but vibrant Evangelical community existed in Cambridge while Simeon was still at Eton! The story of how this community came about is quite remarkable, and sheds light on the entire Evangelical movement of that era, but also has special relevance for the spread of Christianity in Australia. Perhaps more surprisingly, it is a story that is not well known. It is on this story I will focus in this chapter.

2.1. The English Evangelical Revival

We are concerned with Cambridge, but our tale begins at the *other* English university, Oxford, in the year 1729 – a full 30 years before Charles Simeon was born. A small group of men began meeting together for the purpose of devotional study and spurring one another on to pious works. The leaders were two brothers, John and Charles Wesley, and they were eventually joined by a rather shy young man

---

[1]   Gough Whitlam (1916-2014) was Prime Minister from 1972-1975.
[2]   Women were given the right to vote in Australia in 1902.

named George Whitefield. The group attracted a few different nicknames. The one that finally stuck was "Methodist" – originally a term of derision but finally accepted with pride.3

These men were highly disciplined in their practice of prayer, of bible reading, of fasting and so on. A university wit ridiculed them with the following verse:

By rule they eat, by rule they drink,
By rule do all things but think.
Accuse the priests of loose behaviour.
To get more in the laymen's favour.
Method alone must guide 'em all
When themselves "Methodists" they call.4

You will be pleased to learn that Oxford poetry has improved quite a bit since then, but it does show that campus opposition to religious fervour is nothing new. Not that these men were properly "Evangelical" at this stage – not with all their discipline and law keeping. As John Wesley later said, at this time he had 'the faith of a servant, though not that of a son'.5

By the late 1730s, the Wesleys and Whitefield had left Oxford, and we should note that Oxford was happy to be rid of them. They studied and preached, but they were still earnestly seeking for... *something*. The penny dropped for John Wesley in 1738. One evening he was reluctantly listening to a man read from Martin Luther's Preface to Romans:

About a quarter before nine, while he was describing the change which God works in the heart through faith in Christ, I felt my heart strangely warmed. I felt I did trust in Christ, Christ alone for salvation, and an assurance was given me that he had taken away my sins, even mine, and saved me from the law of sin and death.6

3   Henry D Rack, "Holy Club (act. 1729-c.1738)," in *Oxford Dictionary of National Biography* (OUP), http://www.oxforddnb.com.rp.nla.gov.au/view/theme/96375 [accessed 31 May 2015].

4   Anon, The Methodists; an Humorous Burlesque Poem, Address'd to the Revd Mr. Whitefield and His Followers (1739).

5   Henry D Rack, 'Wesley, John (1703-1791)', in *Oxford Dictionary of National Biography*, online edition, May 2010 (OUP, 2004) <http://www.oxforddnb.com .rp.nla.gov.au/view/article/29069> [accessed 5 May 2015].

6   John Wesley, *The Works of the Revd John Wesley*, ed. Joseph Benson (Thomas Blanchard, 1809), I. p 280.

This was a great turning point, and changed the whole character of his ministry. His brother Charles and George Whitfield both underwent remarkably similar conversion experiences around this time, and it is here we might truly label them "Evangelicals". They began preaching up and down the countryside, and on both sides of the Atlantic, and religious revival followed in their wake.[7]

All of this was happening on the fringe of the Anglican Church. But around this time, a number of Anglican clergymen underwent very similar Evangelical conversions, often quite independently of Methodist contact, though they all seemed to find each other pretty quickly. Many of their parishes flourished under Evangelical preaching, and the movement began spreading within the church.[8]

While there were a good number of these Evangelical Anglican leaders, I can only focus on a few. The first plays an especially prominent part in this history. His name was Henry Venn.

2.2.   Henry Venn

Henry Venn was born in Surrey in 1725, and was descended from a line of clergymen that stretched back unbroken to the Reformation. He matriculated to Cambridge in 1742 and won a couple of scholarships, but may have been best remembered there as a star cricket player. His last match was in 1747, playing for Surrey against All England. After the match he literally gave away his cricket bat, for he was getting ordained the following week, and never wanted to hear someone call out the phrase, 'Well struck, Parson!'[9]

In the mid-1750s he was appointed curate of Clapham, and there he came under the influence of John Wesley and George Whitefield, as well as other early Evangelical leaders such as the wealthy merchant John Thornton and Selina, Countess of Huntingdon. He embraced Evangelical beliefs, and was soon after appointed Vicar of Huddersfield

---

7   John F C Harrison, 'Methodism', in *The Oxford Companion to British History*, ed. John Cannon and Robert Crowcroft, 2nd edn (Oxford: OUP, 2015), p 618.

8   See George Balleine, *A History of the Evangelical Party in the Church of England* (London: Church Book Room, 1951). chap.3-5; Kenneth Hylson-Smith, *Evangelicals in the Church of England: 1734-1984* (Edinburgh: T & T Clark, 1988), ch 1-3.

9   Leonard W Cowie, 'Venn, Henry (1725-1797)', in *Oxford Dictionary of National Biography*, online edition, May 2010 (OUP, 2004) <http://www.oxforddnb.com .rp.nla.gov.au/view/article/28184> [accessed 31 May 2015].

in Yorkshire, where he wrote a book called 'The Complete Duty of Man'. It was one of the most influential Evangelical books of the time, running through 20 editions. By this time he himself was recognised as a leader in the movement.[10]

Venn was cheerful, sympathetic and amiable, though often full of passion in the pulpit. He loved his ministry in Huddersfield, but was forced to leave after about 10 years due to problems with his health. He moved to the quiet village of Yelling and became rector of its small church which was just a few miles away from Cambridge. And there we will leave him for a moment while we look at what was happening in the universities.[11]

2.3.   The Universities

The early Evangelicals recognized the importance of the universities. As John Newton noted, the church required:

> ...men who love the truth and who dare to preach it. And since ordination is now scarcely attainable but by those who bring a college testimonial, let us earnestly pray the Lord to pour down his Holy Spirit upon both our Universities that a number and succession of such men may come forth to supply the places...[12]

You will remember that the Methodists had been quite unpopular at Oxford. The Evangelical revivals breaking out all over the country had done nothing to improve opinions, especially since the new movement seemed to appeal most to those of the lowest social rank. There were some Evangelicals at Oxford, but they seemed to survive through something of a "don't ask, don't tell" policy.[13]

In 1769, one of the tutors at St Edmund's College decided to root out the Evangelical miscreants once and for all. He drew up a formal complaint against seven of his students, alleging that they 'talked of regeneration, inspiration, and drawing nigh to God'. An inquiry was held at the University, where they were charged with being enemies of the Church, frequenters of an illegal chapel, and men without learning.

---

10   Cowie, 'Venn'.

11   Cowie, 'Venn'.

12   John Newton, *Memoirs of the Life of the Late Revd William Grimshaw* (London: Baynes and Son, 1825), p 81.

13   Balleine, *History of the Evangelical Party*, pp 124-126.

One accuser stood up and said that they were known to hold to 'the doctrines of Election, Perseverance, and Justification by Faith without Works' and that they were 'connected with reputed Methodists'– including Henry Venn and John Newton. Six of the men were expelled from Oxford, and several more followed in their wake. For the time being, Oxford was largely closed to the Evangelicals.[14]

What about Cambridge? Well, a great deal of anti-evangelical sentiment existed there as well. For example, the Revd John Berridge, who was a fellow at Clare College in the mid-1750s, left to become Vicar of Everton, about 20 miles away. There he 'turned Methodist', and soon came under attack from several Cambridge academics. A small number of students began to ride out to Everton to learn from him, but they soon found that this compromised their situation back at the University.[15]

There were, however, a few signs of life. John Newton took an interest in a number of men at Cambridge. His unpublished diary from the 1770s contains notes such as 'Abraham Clarke met me. He is going to Cambridge... He seems a promising young man.' and 'Mr. Robinson attended the morning meeting with us and prayed; soon after he proceeded to Cambridge.'[16] And amongst the Fellows, Joseph Jowett and Christopher Atkinson were known to have Evangelical leanings. However, there is no evidence of widespread ministry.

We have already noted that Henry Venn became rector of Yelling in 1771, which was just 14 miles away from Cambridge. He soon noted that, 'There are some excellent young men at college, who come to me from the University'.[17] His influence was limited, though, and when he tried to enter his own son into Trinity College, he was refused by the Master and President 'through fear of Methodism'.[18] Young John was finally accepted into another college, but he soon declared 'The very air of Cambridge seems infected by the breath of anti-Christ'.[19] He was later twice passed over for a fellowship, again due to anti-evangelical prejudice.

---

[14] Balleine, *History of the Evangelical Party*, pp 124-126.

[15] John Gascoigne, *Cambridge in the Age of the Enlightenment: Science, Religion and Politics from the Restoration to the French Revolution* (Cambridge: CUP, 1988), p 252.

[16] John Newton Collection, Princeton University, CO199, 29 April 1773, 12 May 1773, 30 January 1775.

[17] Gascoigne, *Cambridge in the Age of the Enlightenment*, p 253.

[18] John Venn, *Annals of a Clerical Family: Being Some Account of the Family and Descendants of William Venn, Vicar of Otterton, Devon, 1600-1621* (Cambridge: CUP, 1904), p 114

[19] Gascoigne, *Cambridge in the Age of the Enlightenment*, p 253.

So things were fairly grim. Yet by the late 1770s, the situation in Cambridge began to turn around for Evangelicals. And the change came from an unlikely source – one of the smallest and poorest colleges.

2.4.   The Magdalene Evangelicals

I've demonstrated the very real difficulties that Evangelicals were facing at the Universities at this time. It is important to appreciate how utterly unlikely the next chapter in the story was. For in the space of just a few years, *three* Evangelicals were elected Fellows at a single Cambridge college.[20]

It is true that the college was Magdalene, one of the smallest and poorest. In the 1770s, the fortunes of Magdalene College were perhaps at their lowest ebb. The student enrolments were in the low single digits, and there were probably only about 4 or 5 Fellows in residence. The rooms were empty, and the great courtyard stood largely silent. Yet its small size served rather to the advantage of the Evangelical triumvirate, for it meant their influence was greatly amplified.[21]

The names of the three young men were Samuel Hey, Henry Jowett and William Farish. As it happened, both Hey and Jowett came from Leeds, and appear to have been influenced by the Methodist movement there.[22]

2.5.   William Farish

Space does not allow me to speak in detail about all three men, but I will spend a few moments discussing William Farish, as he was a remarkable man in his own right, and later became an especially close friend of Simeon's. Farish was born in Carlisle, in the far north of England, and was the son of a Vicar. He was admitted to Magdalene when he was just 16 years old. I've not been able to determine how

---

[20] J D Walsh, 'The Magdalene Evangelicals', *Church Quarterly Review*, 159 (1958).
[21] Peter Cunich and others, *A History of Magdalene College, 1428-1988* (Cambridge: Magdalene College Publications, 1994), pp 179-187, 305-306.
[22] Cunich and others, *History of Magdalene College*, p 186.

Farish became an Evangelical, but he was probably influenced by Henry Jowett, who was his close friend, and Samuel Hey, who was a Fellow.[23]

Farish was an astonishing student. He graduated in 1778 as Senior Wrangler. You might not be familiar with that term, but if you are Senior Wrangler, it basically means that you *won* Cambridge that year – and he was only about 19! He took his MA in 1781 and was immediately elected a fellow of Magdalene, and was also appointed college tutor.[24]

Farish would enjoy an outstanding academic career. He was eventually appointed Professor of Chemistry, Jacksonian Professor of Natural Philosophy, as well as the first President of the Cambridge Philosophical Society. He had a lifelong interest in mechanical devices, and he is credited with developing the drawing technique called "isometric projection", still used by engineers today. He is also recognised as one of the inventors of the modern written examination – so students can make of that what you will![25]

In terms of temperament, he was considered a very serious man, and somewhat placid too. He was not given to great shows of emotion. He was no great orator, though he was popular with the students. Despite his enormous intellect, Simeon described him as possessing a kind of 'heavenly simplicity' which 'delights and edifies every soul.'[26]

If we turn our attention back upon Magdalene College, we noted that by the 1780s there was the Evangelical Triumvirate, Hey, Jowett and Farish, all sitting at the High Table. In 1782, Hey was elected president of the College. With the support of his friends, he set about transforming things. Magdalene soon gained a reputation as '...the general resort of young men seriously impressed with a sense of religion', and the destination of those who desired '...a virtuous rather than a fashionable education.'[27] A great breach had been made in the wall, and Cambridge was no longer quite so hostile to Evangelicals.

Not only did the religious character of the college change, but its academic performance improved dramatically. This was driven by Hey,

---

[23] Anita McConnell, 'Farish, William (1759-1837)', in *Oxford Dictionary of National Biography*, online edition, May 2010 (OUP, 2004).

[24] McConnell, 'Farish'

[25] McConnell, 'Farish'

[26] William Carus, *Memoirs of the Life of the Revd Charles Simeon*, 3rd edn (London: Hatchard and Son, 1847), p 278.

[27] Walsh, 'The Magdalene Evangelicals', p 503-504.

who had spent several years as a tutor prior to his appointment as president. One former student said:

> In this College discipline had been much neglected when the learned and Reverend Samuel Hey was appointed tutor: he immediately began by enforcing a proper degree of attention to study, regularity in attendance on lectures, chapel, etc... To the credit of our tutors... no college, in proportion to its number of pupils, has since that epoch sent out so many men who have distinguished themselves in the University.[28]

Evangelicals began pouring into the college, and it developed a distinctive atmosphere. Another former student fondly recalled his days there with his friends:

> Our terms of intimacy were so familiar we were constantly in the habit of using each other's rooms, books, or whatever either of us wanted, that the other had, without the least ceremony. Pleasanter days than these I never spent; they remind me of that happy state when the first Christians had all things common, parted their goods as each of them had need, and continued daily with one accord eating their bread with gladness and singleness of heart and praising God.[29]

Lest we think the Magdalene Evangelicals were pious killjoys, there was lots of merriment at the college too. From diaries we learn of all sorts of undergraduate mischief, such as letting off fireworks inside the college, scuffles in the corridor, and various practical jokes. One student recalls romping and singing late at night, until Farish came and chased him back to his room. Even serious old Farish let his hair down occasionally; He was acutely embarrassed when a student caught him reading *Tristram Shandy*![30]

2.6. The Elland Clerical Society

Where did this stream of students come from? To answer that, we must return to Henry Venn. Back in 1767, when he was still vicar of Huddersfield, he began a small society with his clerical friends, for the purpose of mutual edification. A few years later, as we have seen, Venn

---

[28] Walsh, 'The Magdalene Evangelicals', p 503-504.
[29] Walsh, 'The Magdalene Evangelicals', p 506-507.
[30] Walsh, 'The Magdalene Evangelicals', p 508.

moved to Yelling, but the quarterly meetings continued, having moved to the Chapel in Elland. It is from here that the association took its name, the Elland Clerical Society – and there are few names more important in the history of Evangelical Anglicanism.[31]

By 1777, the society had determined that the best way for it to promote Evangelicalism in the Church was by sponsoring young men for ordination. They took up subscriptions from amongst the clergy, and one historian described the early subscription list as 'a roll call of the Church's Evangelical leaders'.[32]

The money raised was used to enable poor but talented young men to obtain the education required for ordination. The potential student was first apprenticed to a suitable minister for two years. Assuming all went well, he would be sent to university to obtain his degree, with the Elland Society paying his fees and a pension the whole time.[33]

Which college were these Elland Pensioners to be sent to? Why, to the only college which would welcome them with open arms, Magdalene College in Cambridge, which was run by Revd Samuel Hey – who also happened to be one of the original subscribers to the scheme. The Elland Pensioners entered in great numbers, and dominated the college for a generation.[34]

2.7. *Hull Grammar School*

We have one more stop to make before we finally spend a few minutes looking at Charles Simeon and the "Cambridge connection" with Australia. Now, sometimes the Elland Society would find a promising young man who lacked sufficient schooling even to commence university. What to do in such a situation?

The answer came in the form of Joseph Milner, who was the son of a failed businessman from Leeds. Joseph somehow scraped his way into university, and then astonished everyone by winning the Chancellor's Medal, and against a particularly strong field, too. Milner was simply brilliant. Though weak and asthmatic, he had a quick mind and a

---

[31] A T Yarwood, 'The Making of a Colonial Chaplain: Samuel Marsden and the Elland Society, 1765-93', *Australian Historical Studies*, 16.64 (1975), pp 362-80.

[32] Yarwood, 'Colonial Chaplain', p 367.

[33] Yarwood, 'Colonial Chaplain', pp 367-368.

[34] Walsh, 'The Magdalene Evangelicals', pp 502-503.

phenomenal memory. After his ordination, Milner found himself appointed headmaster of Hull Grammar School in Yorkshire, where he quickly reversed the fortunes of this struggling school.[35]

For a while he was the toast of the town, but then he created a minor scandal by becoming an Evangelical in 1770. Though spurned by the town elite, he was embraced by the common man and he preached to packed churches. And the Elland Society now had a sympathetic school to which they could send their pensioners if they required some polishing up before university.[36]

2.8. Isaac Milner

Joseph Milner had a younger brother called Isaac, and he is the last member of the supporting cast I will introduce. Joseph was able to rescue his brother from a menial job and send him to Cambridge. The brothers were very close all their lives, but they made a startling contrast. While Joseph was frail and asthmatic, Isaac was robust, physically enormous and remarkably strong.[37]

They differed in mental abilities too. While Joseph thrived in languages and history, Isaac excelled in mathematics and science. And while Joseph was brilliant, Isaac was unquestionably a genius. When he finally went to Cambridge a few years later, he swept all before him. He took his B.A. in 1774 and was "Senior Wrangler" and also first in the Smith's Prize.[38]

These were the highest honours Cambridge could award, but his examiners went a step further. When the order of merit was posted, they appended the word "*Incomparabilis*" to his name. He was truly in a class of his own. He went on to enjoy a dazzling academic career: Elected fellow of the Royal Society, appointed inaugural Jacksonian Professor of Natural Philosophy, and also appointed Lucasian Professor

35 D Bruce Hindmarsh, 'Milner, Joseph (1745-1797)', in *Oxford Dictionary of National Biography*, online edition, May 2010 (OUP, 2004) <http://www.oxforddnb.com. rp.nla.gov.au/view/article/18792>. [accessed 31 May 2015]

36 Hindmarsh 'Milner, Joseph'; Walsh, 'The Magdalene Evangelicals', p. 501.

37 Keven C Knox, 'Milner, Isaac (1750-1820)', in *Oxford Dictionary of National Biography*, online edition, May 2010 (OUP, 2004) <http://www.oxforddnb.com. rp.nla.gov.au/view/article/18788>. [accessed 31 May 2015].

38 Knox, 'Milner, Isaac'.

of Mathematics – the same chair held by Isaac Newton and Stephen Hawking.[39]

Milner was not an Evangelical when he entered College, but it seems likely he was converted through the influence of his brother and Joseph Jowett, who was his very close friend. Milner was widely read and a superb conversationalist, and tended to dominate the social circles in which he moved.[40] His friends found him kind-hearted and amiable, yet his enemies encountered a formidable and ruthless debater. Simeon once noted that Milner had 'crushed his adversary to atoms' in a certain controversy.[41]

Milner was elected fellow of Queens' College in 1776, and then president in 1788 – a post he held for 32 years. He set about transforming Queens', and his brilliance and dominating manner made him almost impossible to resist. He carefully expunged the college of undesirables, and replaced them with sound Evangelicals. One historian even described him as 'the evangelical church militant'.[42] Within a few years Queens' had surpassed Magdalene as the centre of Evangelical influence at Cambridge.[43]

2.9.   Charles Simeon

It is time for a few brief words on the subject of this book, Charles Simeon. My purpose is just to show how he connected into the existing Evangelical community at Cambridge.

Simeon was born in Berkshire in 1759, the son of a prosperous attorney. He was descended from vicars on his father's side, and two archbishops on his mother's side. He attended Eton and was not popular with his schoolmates, earning the nickname "Chin Simeon" because of his profile. He later said that Eton had done nothing to inspire any religious awareness in him.[44]

---

39   Knox, 'Milner, Isaac'.

40   James Stephen, *Essays in Ecclesiastical Biography*, 4th edn (London: Longman, Green, Longman and Roberts, 1860), pp 566-572.

41   Carus, *Memoirs of the Life*, p 265.

42   Gascoigne, *Cambridge in the Age of the Enlightenment*, p 254.

43   Walsh, 'The Magdalene Evangelicals', p 508.

44   Leonard W Cowie, 'Simeon, Charles (1759-1836)', in *Oxford Dictionary of National Biography*, online edition, Oct 2005 (OUP, 2004) <http://www.oxforddnb.com.rp.nla.gov.au/view/article/25559> [accessed 31 May 2015].

Simeon was admitted to King's College, Cambridge in 1779 at the age of 18. The story of his subsequent conversion is well known. He was informed soon after his arrival that he would be required to take communion several weeks later, and the thought filled him with dread. Was he worthy to participate in such a holy event? He read several tracts and books, and came to understand that his sin had been transferred to 'the sacred head of Jesus'. When he finally took communion, he was able to write, 'At the Lord's table in our chapel I had the sweetest access to God through my blessed Saviour'.[45]

Yet things were not so neat. For the first three years after his conversion, he had little contact with anyone who shared his religious convictions. At the same time that Magdalene College was blossoming into an Evangelical powerhouse, Simeon was struggling to figure out his religion almost entirely on his own.[46]

Shortly after being elected Fellow of Kings in 1782, Simeon began attending church at St Edward's, where Christopher Atkinson was vicar. As we noted before, Atkinson was a fellow of Trinity, and also an Evangelical. When Atkinson realised Simeon's religious convictions, he introduced him to John Venn, and Simeon at last found a kindred spirit. A few weeks later, John Venn took Simeon over to Yelling, to meet his father. Simeon stayed for 12 hours in conversation with Henry Venn, and later wrote:

> O what an acquisition was this! In this aged minister I found a father, an instructor, and a most bright example: and I shall have reason to adore my God to all eternity for the benefit of his acquaintance.[47]

Simeon was soon introduced to the entire Evangelical circle at Cambridge, and made a strong impression on everyone. He and Farish became especially close. Berridge noted in 1782 that 'Mr Simeon... has just made his appearance in the Christian hemisphere.'[48] Henry Venn wrote to a friend, 'I have good news to send you from Cambridge – Mr Simeon is made for great usefulness.'[49] Milner was initially cautious, but soon became '...convinced of his truly Christian spirit and

45 Cowie, 'Simeon, Charles (1759-1836)'.
46 Carus, *Memoirs of the Life*, p 11.
47 Carus, *Memoirs of the Life*, p 23.
48 Gascoigne, *Cambridge in the Age of the Enlightenment*, pp 254-255.
49 Gascoigne, *Cambridge in the Age of the Enlightenment*, pp 254-255.

usefulness, and of his unreserved devotedness to the glory of God' and he later described Simeon as a 'dear friend'.[50]

Simeon was ordained in 1782, and through his father's connections he was appointed Vicar of Holy Trinity church in Cambridge. It was not a popular decision, but over time more and more of the Evangelicals now coming to Cambridge found their way to his church, and sat beneath his preaching. He was concerned about the lack of specialized training for ordinands, so he set up sermon classes in his college rooms. He also established weekly conversation parties (at first attended only by Magdalene men!) where he instructed students in points of practical Christianity. As these disciples went out and took up their parishes, his influence grew enormous. One contemporary historian noted that his authority 'extended from Cambridge to the most remote corners of England' and that 'his real sway in the Church was far greater than that of any primate.'[51]

But we will leave this story for now as this will be the subject of much of the rest of this volume.

2.10.   *The Cambridge Evangelicals and Australia*

All of the pieces are now in play: the Elland Clerical Society, Hull Grammar School, and the colleges of Magdalene and Queens'. I have called this the *Cambridge Connection*, and it proved a highly successful system for pumping Evangelical influence into the Church, with around 60 ordinands delivered by 1800.[52] And of particular interest to us, it was the Cambridge Connection that supplied Australia with its clergymen in the earliest colonial period.

Let us look at Richard Johnson, the first chaplain. He was not an Elland Pensioner, however he did go to Hull Grammar School, and later on entered Magdalene College. Chalk one up for the Cambridge Connection.[53]

---

50   Carus, *Memoirs of the Life*, pp 164-166.
51   Cowie, 'Simeon, Charles (1759-1836)'.
52   Walsh, 'The Magdalene Evangelicals', p 509.
53   Kenneth Cable, 'Johnson, Richard (1753-1827)', in *Australian Dictionary of Biography*, National Centre of Biography, online edition (Australian National University, 1967) <http://adb.anu.edu.au/biography/johnson-richard-2275/text2921>. [accessed online 31 May 2015]

The second colonial chaplain was a little known fellow called John Crowther, who was shipwrecked on the way to Sydney and never arrived. Like Johnson, he was educated at Hull Grammar School and then entered Magdalene, graduating in 1788. Another one![54]

At last we come to Samuel Marsden, and here we take the trifecta. An Elland Pensioner, educated at Hull Grammar School, and then sent on to Magdalene College, before setting off for his long and famous career in NSW.[55]

Now, things changed a little after 1800, with a fair number of men being ordained for the colony without degrees. Magdalene supplied just three more clergymen to Australia over the next 50 years.[56] Things were better at Queens, with 11 men ending up clerics on Australian soil over the same period.[57] I've not done the research to determine what proportion of these latter graduates were Evangelical. However, it seems certain that most would have felt the influence of Simeon.

Charles Simeon – it is hard to avoid his name when speaking about Cambridge at this time. Given his enormous contributions, it is probably appropriate that his is the 'one great name' that is recalled. But I hope I have demonstrated that the *Cambridge Connection* of the Elland Clerical Society, Hull Grammar School and the Evangelical Colleges both preceded Simeon and also provided the context for his early ministry. Ultimately, the *Cambridge Connection* and Simeon were not in competition. Rather, they worked together to supply a generation of Evangelical Clergymen to the Anglican Church, in both England and Australia.

---

54 Church of England Clergy Database, Person ID: 10406
55 A T Yarwood, 'Marsden, Samuel (1765-1838)', in *Australian Dictionary of Biography*, National Centre of Biography, online edition (Australian National University, 1967) <http://adb.anu.edu.au/biography/marsden-samuel-2433/text3237>.   [accessed online 31 May 2015]
56 These were William Clay, James Lang and George Despard. See Leonie Cable, *The Cable Clerical Index*, online at <http://anglicanhistory.org/aus/cci/>.
57 These were Walter Bradbury, William Dudley, Thomas Fenner, George Johnstone, William Lyde, Michael Mayers, Charles Morse, Edward Nixon, John Seaman, Richard Taylor and Charles Woodward. See the *Cable Clerical Index*.

3. Charles Simeon's Influence on Samuel Marsden's Chaplaincy in New South Wales – *David Pettett*

Fellow of King's College and Vicar of Holy Trinity Church, Cambridge, (1782-1836) the influence of the Revd Charles Simeon on the early colony of New South Wales cannot be overestimated. Through his 'intimate friend', Simeon's ideas of personal Christian piety, pastoral oversight, magisterial function, the order of society and missionary endeavour made their way to the antipodes.[1] The Revd Samuel Marsden became a student at Magdalene College, Cambridge in late 1790. Magdalene at the time was an Evangelical hotbed.[2] Marsden attended Simeon's 'conversation parties' in his rooms at King's.[3] Here Marsden learnt the art of expository preaching from the man whose passion was to train young Evangelical ministers. The two established and maintained a correspondence throughout their lives.[4] Simeon accompanied Marsden on both his departures from England, the first in 1793 when he travelled with him through the Isle of White and the second in 1809 when they parted company in Marsden's cabin at the last minute as the Pilot was leaving the ship.[5]

To understand Simeon's high regard for Marsden we read in his correspondence that in early 1791 Simeon had recommended Marsden not only for the chaplaincy in New South Wales but also for the chaplaincy in Bengal.[6] These recommendations came at a time when Marsden was only newly arrived in Cambridge.

---

[1] Carus describes Marsden as his 'intimate friend': William Carus, *Memoirs of the Life of the Revd Charles Simeon*, 3rd edn (London: Hatchard and Son, 1847), p 81.

[2] See Chapter 2 for more details.

[3] See Abner Brown, *Recollections of the Conversation Parties of the Revd Charles Simeon* (London: Hamilton, Adams, & Co., 1863).

[4] The Simeon Archives in Ridley Hall, Cambridge hold three letters, two from Marsden to Simeon, 9 July 1792 and 26 April 1794, and one from Simeon to Marsden, 10 November 1835. In this last letter Simeon mentions previous correspondence between the pair that is not in the archives.

[5] Simeon, 'Letter to Samuel Marsden', 10 November 1835. Simeon Archives: Ridley Hall.

[6] See a letter from Charles Grant to Charles Simeon dated 17 March, 1791 in the Simeon Archives in Ridley Hall, Cambridge. Grant informs Simeon that the matter of Marsden had been raised with the Archbishop of Canterbury who expressed his opinion that Marsden had been too short a time at Cambridge (just a few months!) and that he 'was too young, to be sent to Botany Bay; and that the same reasons applied more strongly against his now going to Bengal.'

The great affection with which Marsden held Simeon, over and above other significant mentors and patrons, is evidenced by the fact that Marsden named his first born son Charles Simeon. Following Charles' tragic death at age three in August 1801, having been thrown from a chase in front of the family home, Marsden also named his third son, born after his older sibling's death, Charles Simeon. An aboriginal man at Marsden's Mamre farm was also known as Simeon. Marsden's habits of Christian piety mimicked those of his mentor. Marsden's preaching in the colony of New South Wales was entirely shaped by Simeon. Marsden's understanding of the role of magistrates took its shape from Simeon's practices. Marsden accepted Simeon's understanding of the ordering of society. This ultimately saw Marsden at odds with the early steps in the colony towards an egalitarian Australian society. Marsden followed Simeon's ideas of voluntarism when it came to supporting mission.

While the influence of Simeon cannot be overestimated, at the same time the unique complexity of the situation in which Marsden operated, likewise, cannot be overestimated. The establishment of the colony of New South Wales was a great experiment of the Enlightenment. The English made the decision to send men and women who needed improvement to a land that also needed improvement if it was going to support husbandry for a western culture.

Interactions with the Eora people and differing expectations of his role as Chaplain are just some of the complexities Marsden worked with. Each challenged his way of doing ministry and the ideas of Christian piety he brought with him from England which were informed by his Evangelical background. To complicate matters, Marsden brought with him a form of Christianity that was changing the way the Church of England operated. The Evangelical Awakening had given rise to groups within the Church of England which were organised and politically savvy. Marsden was part of this. We should have no surprise therefore when we later see him organising mission strategy and being heavily involved in the politics of the colony.

3.1. Simeon's Influence – Preaching

Study of Marsden's sermons shows his ultimate vision was not simply for an improved society in Enlightenment terms but for an eschatological one informed by Evangelical theology. While Marsden wanted to see the people of the colony behaving well and seeking the safety and prosperity of all its people he also wanted to see men and women making sure of a place in heaven. He faced the great difficulty of preaching about another place that was not of this world, at a time when the focus for many people was on making a fortune of material wealth in a new colony. He preached of another world to men and women who were striving to make their fortune and/or their freedom in this temporal world.

One hearer of Marsden's eschatological focused sermons observed a certain familiarity with the words. The Wesleyan minister the Revd Walter Lawry is recorded as saying of Marsden that, 'On Sunday he reads the liturgy like a man half asleep, and then uniformly serves up one of Simeon's skeletons with very little lean flesh about it.'[7] Simeon published sermon outlines as a means of teaching young preachers exegetical preaching. These outlines became known as 'skeletons'. Lawry complained that Marsden just dished up skeletons of sermons to his congregation with little of his own work in them. Lawry's comment is pivotal in the study of Marsden's preaching. My research has shown that his criticism is justified to a certain degree. Marsden has used Simeon's outlines extensively and somewhat slavishly.[8] Where Marsden

---

[7] Bill Wannan, *Very Strange Tales: The Turbulent Times of Samuel Marsden* (Melbourne: Lansdowne, 1962), p 176. Wannan gives no reference for this quotation. A second criticism of Marsden's preaching may be implied from Archdeacon Scott's comment on ministry in general throughout the colony that he 'found the Services administered much more after the manner of a Methodist Chapel than of the Church ... Their sermons are delivered extempore, or at least unwritten with a Bible in their hand *full of bookstrings*, placed in the texts they intend to use by way of illustration ... and they usually continue an hour & sometimes more delivering the most unconnected sentences'. Scott to Archdeacon A Hamilton, 3 March 1827, SPG Archives, Australia letters no.5, cited in A.T. Yarwood, *Samuel Marsden: The Great Survivor* (Carlton, Vic.: Melbourne University Press, 1977), p 262. Despite Yarwood's comment on p 263 that 'Much of this description applied to Marsden' and our knowledge that Marsden did, on occasion, preach extempore, in the main he wrote out his sermons (as Yarwood acknowledges) in full. That Marsden may have preached for 'an hour or more' is disproved by the fact of the length of his written sermons which, at about 3,000 words being their normal length, would have taken about 20 minutes to preach. Of course the possibility remains that Marsden may have added to his written sermons as he delivered them.

[8] There are 135 Marsden sermons or parts of sermons in various collections around the world. The largest collection is in Moore Theological College, Sydney with 98 sermons. The second largest is the family collection, currently in the possession of the Revd Samuel Marsden of Cornwall, UK with 25 sermons. Study of these sermons shows that where Marsden has used a Simeon skeleton, which he has done in approximately two thirds of all the extant sermons, he invariably copies out the first few paragraphs of the outline word for word.

has not used a Simeon outline the form of his sermon follows closely the form he learned from the Master.

In his Evangelical upbringing there were other masters Marsden also learned from: Samuel Stones,[9] Miles Atkinson,[10] and Joseph Milner.[11] Marsden's biographer, A T Yarwood, believes the content and

---

9   In October 1787, at the age of twenty one, Marsden began his formal studies under the tutelage of the Revd Samuel Stones, the Curate of Rawdon Chapel and a member of the Elland Society. The Methodist preacher, John Wesley, described Stones in his journal as 'a truly pious and active man' (John Wesley, *The Works of Revd John Wesley* (New York: J & J Harper, 1826), IV. pp 416-417.) Other than this we know very little of Stones. There are no published sermons of his to compare with Marsden and no biographer or other commentator makes reference to his preaching content or style. There is also no reference in the *Oxford Dictionary of National Biography* for Stones.

10   Atkinson was the Vicar of Kippax, minister of St. Paul's and Lecturer of the Parish Church in Leeds. Marsden sometimes stayed with him during his time as an Elland Probationer and also, with his family, during his return to England between 1807 and 1809. Marsden regularly wrote to Atkinson often seeking advice. After receiving his first grant of land in October 1794, Marsden wrote to Atkinson asking if this was an appropriate course. After putting the question to a meeting of the Elland Society Atkinson wrote back with the meeting's unanimous approval. Atkinson was the Treasurer of the Elland Society.

11   Milner was the Master of Hull Grammar which Marsden attended in 1788. A comparison of Marsden's preaching style with Milner's is helpful here. Their styles differ significantly. A sermon on Genesis 18:9 will serve as an illustration. A sermon by Milner on this passage is published in his own 'Practical Sermons' (Joseph Milner, *Practical Sermons* (London: Cadell & Davies, 1821), pp 209-224) and there is one by Marsden in the Moore College collection on the same passage. In his sermon, Milner speaks of the faithfulness of Abraham and concentrates on the role of those who are, 'Masters of families'. Marsden, following Simeon's outline also brings this focus telling his hearers that Abraham, 'eminently excelled in the observance of what may be called family religion.' But where Milner continues on this theme throughout his sermon Marsden brings in the roles of magistrates as ministers of God and uses Abraham as an example of authority, 'whether it be official, or personal, civil or religious.' Marsden also speaks at length on the 'violation of the Sabbath' which he describes as, 'a common sin amongst us' which 'many imagine ... [to be] a sin of little consequence' but declares 'there is no sin with all its attendant evil [that will] ruin men's souls so much as this.' Sabbath breaking, and its attendant consequences, is a constant theme in Marsden's preaching. Of the 98 sermons in the Moore College collection thirteen have warnings about the issue of Sabbath breaking. Whereas Milner has remained consistent with his theme on the role of Masters of Families, Marsden has allowed his thoughts to drift onto one of his favourite themes, irrespective of the scriptural passage he has been preaching on. While this may be indicative of the pastoral situation Marsden found himself in, as a preacher who has a high regard for the Bible, Milner shows himself to be the one who more faithfully follows an Evangelical tradition by constantly applying the biblical text rather than drifting off into a favourite subject.

style of Marsden's religious message 'bears the clear stamp of the great Leeds preacher' (referring to Atkinson).[12] It is hard to agree with this assessment. While there are similarities in their style, the clear stamp on Marsden's preaching has been Simeon. As noted above, Marsden has copied out slabs of Simeon's outlines in his own sermons.[13]

It would be true to say that Marsden has used Simeon's outlines extensively and somewhat slavishly. In his Introduction to *Horae Homileticae* Simeon speaks of the advice that had been given to young preachers of his day 'to transcribe printed sermons for a season, till they have attained an ability to compose their own'. He lamented 'that this advice has been too strictly followed: for, when they have once formed this habit, they find it very difficult to relinquish it'.[14] No doubt Simeon would have been disappointed that Marsden was not able to break this habit throughout his life. In the Moore College collection of 98 sermons almost three quarters (73 of 98) have used a Simeon outline. In most of these sermons, Marsden has simply copied out the outline word for word for the first few paragraphs. As he goes on, however, he moves away more from the outline and develops his own thinking. Sermon Three in the Moore College collection is typical of how Marsden has used Simeon. The sermon has a total of 3,326 words of which 2,129 are Marsden's own. That is, almost two thirds of the sermon is in Marsden's own words. However, in some cases the differences from Simeon's outline are very minor. For example in the first paragraph of the sermon Marsden used the word 'able', where Simeon had used 'enabled'.

Another example is where Simeon spoke about eternal redemption using the word 'us', whereas Marsden has replaced 'us' with the phrase 'all that believe in his name' making it clear he believed that eternal redemption was not just for 'us' who happen to be listening to this sermon, but only for those who 'believe'. Marsden did not want his hearers to think that salvation was universally available, so he has made

---

[12] Yarwood, *Great Survivor*, p 10.

[13] Yarwood also mistakenly believes the inspiration for Marsden's sermon following the death of the Judge Advocate, Ellis Bent, for which Macquarie gave Marsden a public dressing down, came from the Revd Peter Peckard, Master of Magdalene College, Cambridge, at the time Marsden was a student there. This is certainly not the case. It is clear that the sermon relied on Simeon's outline for the passage, 2 Chronicles 29:10-11.

[14] Charles Simeon, *Horae Homileticae or Discourses (in the Form of Skeletons) upon the Whole Scriptures* (London: Richard Watts, 1819), I. p iv.

it clear that there is an action required to avail oneself of 'eternal redemption' and that is to 'believe in his name.' These differences of theological emphasis are highlighted in the following quotation from Marsden's Sermon 3:6[15] where he has slavishly followed Simeon's outline but has added his own words which are underlined:

> But when we see that he did rise from the dead, and did ascend up into heaven in the presence of his disciples, and did send down the Holy Ghost according to his word of promise to bear testimony concerning him, there is no room left for doubt, but that he actually did give his life a ransom for sinners, and we are perfectly assured that his offering was accepted of the Father, and that by his obedience unto death he hath wrought out eternal redemption for [us] all that believe in his name. Hence St. Paul boldly asks who shall condemn us? Etc

In a small way, Marsden's sermons show clear evidence of Enlightenment language, where Simeon's outlines do not. However, for Marsden this is only a style of language usage. It does not denote a departure from his Evangelical theological position. For example in Sermon 2:11 Marsden says,

> He came to give us rational and worthy notions of that Being we are obliged to adore, & is most properly adopted to raise our natures to the greatest improvement they are capable of.

This sermon has not used Simeon's outline on the passage which is Luke 2:10. Sermon 33 is on the same passage from Luke 2:10 and has used Simeon's outline. The words 'rational ... notions' and 'raise our natures to the greatest improvement' are not in Sermon 33 and are terms Simeon has not used in his outline. This highlights that when he is not sitting under the direct influence of his mentor, copying paragraphs from Simeon, Marsden's language has taken on an Enlightenment hue. It is not a theological change but a change of language which probably indicates the influences which were on Marsden in the Colony. The thrust of Sermon Two makes it very clear that despite his Enlightenment language Marsden's theology has not changed. As he nears the end of the sermon on the last page he speaks of a standard Evangelical belief that a person can only enter heaven by

---

15 References to Marsden's sermons in this chapter are to the Moore College collection unless otherwise indicated. The sermon number is referenced first followed by a colon and the page number so that Sermon three page seven would be Sermon 3:7 or simply 3:7.

the blood of Jesus. The exhortation is couched in his normal harsh language towards the end of his sermons as he declares:

> ... nothing that is unholy and unclean can enter the kingdom of God. There are no drunkards there, no unclean persons, no profane persons, none but such as have washed their robes and made them white in the blood of the Lamb.[16]

His point is that heaven is populated not by those who might have 'rational notions' nor by personal improvement, but by being washed in the blood of Jesus which has by God's grace made them white. This is straight up and down Evangelical theology. His use of the word 'improvement' throughout his sermons is instructive. In the 98 sermons in the Moore College collection Marsden has used the word 'improvement' in a moral sense hardly at all. The word occurs a total of 23 times and almost always has the meaning of 'improving a subject', that is, expanding or explaining the subject matter.[17]

Where Marsden uses the word in a moral sense it is not used to call his hearers to a mere improvement of living. For example, on the right use of the Sabbath, Marsden says that if the people had used the Sabbath Day aright they themselves would have had a moral improvement to the glory of God:

> Have we not also enjoyed many Sabbaths and ordinances in which God hath promised his blessing. These might have been turned to good account for our improvement and the glory of God. (19:4)

In this passage Marsden wants people to keep the Sabbath so that the Colony will become a better place to live with moral, upright citizens, 'for our improvement'. His focus, however, goes beyond this temporal benefit of an improved society. He declares that the 'improvement' of keeping the Sabbath, will be to 'the glory of God'. Here we see Marsden's eschatological focus. His sermons do not simply make a call to civilisation, or even to an elevation of rational thought as opposed to revelation. In his preaching there is emphasis on the call of the gospel, the account all people will one day give to the Sovereign God as judge of all for everything they have ever done and said. Marsden did not believe that the state of human kind could be improved without the

---

[16] Sermon 2:16

[17] For example: 'By way of improvement let us enquire.' (Sermon 2:13) 'We shall now conclude this subject by way of improvement.' (Sermon 30:22) 'We shall conclude with considering what improvement we should make of this subject.' (Sermon 36:14)

intervention of God. His sermons include an emphasis on the work of the Holy Spirit to change lives. For example in Sermon 33:20 he says, 'if you are his people he will dwell in your hearts. Your bodies will become his temple thru the Holy Ghost.' Again in Sermon 80:14, emphasising that there is no growth or improvement in the human condition without the inner working of God, Marsden says, 'The word must come to us in power & in the Holy Ghost, or it will come in vain, but when applied to us by the Spirit it shall teach us plainly of the Father.' On the subject of whether or not a person can be assured of entrance into heaven Marsden emphasised that even this work is not achieved by improvement of morals or by rational thinking but:

> The righteousness of Christ is imputed to every believing soul in order to justification, and the Holy Ghost is sent down from heaven to sanctify his nature and to render him meet for the blessed inheritance.[18]

Theologically Marsden, being a product of the Evangelical movement, followed his mentor and the general Evangelical style, closely. Even where his language has taken on an Enlightenment hue, Marsden continued to express an Evangelical theological position.

When it comes to points of application Marsden tends to be more direct and harsh than Simeon. To be fair, Simeon has written outlines that he expects others to use in their own preaching and therefore, unlike Marsden, he is not speaking into a specific pastoral context. Sermon 70:3 serves as a good example of Marsden's directness. He says,

> many glory in their shame or what ought to be their shame. Some live in drunkenness & ludeness *(sic)*, others in falsehood & dishonesty, others in pride & envy, and others in malice and revenge and under the influence of every sinful passion. And do not these sins shew that such persons are far from God and strangers to his presence, and his fear is not before their eyes.

In his outline of this passage Simeon has the same litany of sin but he has prefaced it by saying, 'it is not improbable that some live in open sin' whereas Marsden has said, 'It is well know[n] that many in this assembly live in the habitual commission of open and known sins.'[19]

---

18 Sermon 88:15-16
19 Sermon 70:2

Simeon's appointment by the Bishop of Ely as Vicar of Holy Trinity, Cambridge was the beginning of many years of tensions between Simeon and his parishioners. Through it all Simeon's memoirs show that he constantly worked with the situation, seeking God's guidance and blessing. When he observed that, because of locked pews in the Church only half the number of people as might be expected were able to attend Divine Service, Simeon prayed that God would give them a double blessing. It was his hope that by this double blessing the effects of his ministry would not be diminished by the smaller number present because of the locked pews. It is easy to imagine this attitude to ministry was something that Marsden took on board and shaped his attitude in the face of the hardships and opposition he encountered in his own ministry in the Colony. Marsden followed throughout his life the habit that Simeon established of rising at 4 a.m. each day to pray.[20]

3.2. Simeon's Influence – Magistracy

Marsden's decision to take up a position as a magistrate may well have been guided by Simeon's teachings and practice. Michael Gladwin has pointed out, 'Marsden's clerical and intellectual formation coincided precisely with a dramatic expansion of Evangelical activism in the social and political spheres.'[21] Simeon was not only actively preparing young men for Evangelical ministry, but also, as a university fellow, was in a position to exercise authority over disorderly behaviour of students and townsmen. In his memoirs, Simeon declared that he saw it his duty to be firm over disorderly behaviour.[22] Simeon did not promote the idea of clergy taking a role as a magistrate, but his writings are filled with ideas of the importance of civil order and the role of the magistrate in this. Simeon believed that the magistrate's role was to ensure civil order and

---

[20] J B Marsden, *Memoirs of the Life and Labours of the Revd Samuel Marsden, of Parramatta, Senior Chaplain of New South Wales: And of His Early Connexion with the Missions to New Zealand and Tahiti* (London: Religious Tract Society, 1858), p 73. 'Mr Marsden rose early, generally at four o'clock during the summer; and the morning hours were spent in his study.'

[21] Michael Gladwin, 'Marsden's Generals: Metropolitan Roots of Marsden's Mission', in *Launching Marsden's Mission. The Beginnings of the Church Missionary Society in New Zealand, Viewed from New South Wales*, ed. by Peter Bolt and David Pettett (Latimer Trust, 2014), p 15.

[22] Carus, *Memoirs of the Life*, pp 89-93.

for this the magistrate held an appointment from God.[23] Marsden followed this line of reasoning. In Sermon 63:3-4 Marsden declared:

> The power that is given us, of whatever kind it be is bestowed for this end, and to God alone we are responsible for the use of it. Magistrates are invested with it by him and are therefore called his ministers.

Simeon and Marsden agree that magistrates are invested with power from God. In the Moore College collection there are seven sermons in which Marsden speaks of the role of magistrates. In each of these he speaks of the duty of members of a civilised society, under God, to obey magistrates. Christians are to keep in mind that they are to 'be subject to principalities and powers, and to obey magistrates'. In words that give some insight into how Marsden may have justified his own harshness as a magistrate he says, 'The office of magistrates is to do all in their power for the suppression of iniquity.'[24] As much as these words may be a self-justification, Marsden believed that the work of a magistrate was God's work for the good ordering of society. In Sermon 27:1 he speaks of the Apostle Paul's address to Christians at Rome where:

> He points out to them several both social and relative duties, enjoins upon them a peaceable and quiet subjection to earthly governors as God's ministers appointed to protect the lives and properties of subjects and to punish those who dare invade the rights of civil society. Therefore says the apostle the civil magistrate is a minister to the[m] for good, a revenger to execute wrath upon him that doeth evil.

In speaking of the formation of Israel under Moses Marsden points out how God also commanded the appointment of judges and makes the statement, 'The institution of magistrates and judges is a necessary part of every well-ordered government.'[25] Simeon's concern in his outline on this passage of scripture is to do with the fallout from the French Revolution. He declares,

> We have witnessed the destruction of all constituted authorities, and the utter annihilation of all established laws. We have beheld licentiousness stalking with the cap of liberty, and ferocious despotism, under the name of equality, spreading desolation with an undiscriminating hand [Note: At the time of the French Revolution.]. But, blessed be God, it is not thus with Britain: I pray

---

23 See Gladwin, 'Marsden's Generals', pp 13-30.
24 Sermon 23:1, 2 & 4.
25 Sermon 56:4.

God it never may be.[26]

This is a telling description of Simeon's view. Licentiousness, liberty, despotism and equality have destroyed 'all constituted authorities'. This is a view notable amongst a number of English Evangelicals of the time. It speaks of a belief that God has ordained a clearly hierarchical society where there are those in authority and those who obey and where there is no such thing as liberty and equality. While Marsden does not take up any reference to the French Revolution in his sermon, he does emphasise the due ordering of society as an ordinance of God. He declares that, 'The same Apostle writing to the Romans he exhorts them to be subject to the powers that be in authority, for there is no power but of God, for the powers that be are ordained of God.'[27]

3.3.   Simeon's Influence – Mission

John Bennett has written on the subject of how Simeon reconciled his Anglican churchmanship with his involvement in missionary efforts outside the established church. He says that, 'Reconciling the tension between his regular Anglican churchmanship and the voluntarism of Evangelical missionary efforts is key to understanding Simeon's mission legacy.'[28] This legacy was inherited by Marsden. In part it explains why Marsden abandoned any effective efforts to reach the Aboriginal people of the colony and moved, instead, to concentrate his missionary efforts towards the people of New Zealand.

Bennett points out that Simeon's Evangelicalism predisposed him to be favourable towards the burgeoning missionary movement typified by its voluntarism. '[Simeon] reconciled his voluntary acts with his churchmanship through a commitment to general order in society, of which ecclesiastical order was a subset.'[29] Simeon believed that if voluntarism did not disturb social or ecclesiastical order, it was to be encouraged and welcomed. Marsden followed this line of thought. In

---

[26]   Charles Simeon, *Horae Homileticae or Discourses (in the Form of Skeletons) upon the Whole Scriptures* (London: Richard Watts, 1819), III. p 113. (Outline 283). The words in square brackets are in the original.

[27]   Sermon 56:4.

[28]   John Bennett, 'The Legacy of Charles Simeon', *International Bulletin of Missionary Research* <https://www.questia.com/magazine/1G1-15435589/the-legacy-of-charles-simeon>.

[29]   John Bennett, 'Charles Simeon and the Evangelical Missionary Movement. A Study of Voluntarism and Church Mission Tensions' (unpublished Ph.D. Thesis, Edinburgh, 1992).

Sermon 34 in the Moore College collection Marsden encourages his hearers to join with the missionary societies in the work of declaring the gospel in foreign lands:

> It is my most ardent wish (& that of my colleagues) to inspire you with a zeal for the salvation of a lost world, to call upon you (as a small branch of the British Nation) to imitate the example of the wisest and best men in the ~~British~~ Empire and join with them in so great a work, as the building of the walls of Jerusalem.[30]

Marsden did not see this voluntarism as a disturbance to society but rather a duty of nation and empire.

As an Anglican clergyman, responsible for the Christian care of the people of New South Wales, Marsden came under heavy criticism for his neglect of the Aboriginal people. The criticism came to a head on 4 January 1817 when a letter appeared in the *Sydney Gazette* under the signature of '*Philo Free*'.[31] The letter accused those involved in the South Seas mission of introducing alcohol and guns to their own financial advantage while neglecting the native population of New South Wales. Marsden, believing himself to be the object of the criticism in the letter, instituted criminal and civil action against the author which he won.

The circumstances surrounding the *Philo Free* letter highlight the issue of voluntarism and Anglican churchmanship. Marsden as an Anglican clergyman was subject to the principles, practices and discipline of the Church of England. Yet he held that he was going to New South Wales not bound by the strictures of his Anglican heritage. He believed he had a commission from God to preach the gospel to the people of the South Seas and prayed that, 'the end of my going may be answered in the Conversion of many poor Souls'.[32] He saw the establishment of the colony as the providential means of taking the gospel to the people of the South Seas. He carried with him the hopes and expectations of key Evangelicals that he would share with the Revd Richard Johnson (the first chaplain to the colony) the title of Apostle to the South Seas.[33] These Evangelical expectations of the conversion of lost souls and of an apostolic ministry to the South Seas were different from those expectations expressed by government authorities. Colonial officials expected Marsden

---

[30] Sermon 34:24; the strike-through is in the original.
[31] *Sydney Gazette* 4 January 1817, p 3. Electronic reproduction available at <http://nla.gov.au/nla.news-page493206>.
[32] Samuel Marsden, *Diary – 1793-1794*. Mitchell Library, C245. Entry dated 27 July, 1793.
[33] John Newton, 'Letter to the Revd Richard Johnson', 24 May 1793. *NSWHR* Vol 2 p 27.

and Johnson before him to confine their preaching to moral subjects.[34] They expected he would limit his ministry to the moral improvement of the people of the colony. This included the aboriginal people who, on the establishment of the colony had very quickly become an urbanised people.[35] Yet Marsden's Evangelical convictions led him to be involved in missionary efforts beyond the bounds of his role as Senior Chaplain to the colony of New South Wales. Like his mentor, Charles Simeon, Marsden reconciled his voluntary acts in the establishment and ongoing support of the mission to New Zealand, with his churchmanship through a commitment to the good order of society both in New Zealand and New South Wales.

He constantly called people to be upright citizens, respecting law and order. In speaking on Paul's letter to the Romans, Marsden says, 'He ... enjoins upon them a peaceable and quiet subjection to earthly governors as God's ministers appointed to protect ... the rights of civil society.'[36] For Marsden this call was an essential element of his missionary efforts. He saw no distinction between his role as an Anglican clergyman and his role as a leader of missionary enterprise. Both roles sought to bring people into a well ordered society as they responded to the claims of the gospel in their lives.

3.4. Conclusions

This chapter has examined the influence of Charles Simeon over the colony of New South Wales through his protégé, the Revd Samuel Marsden in Marsden's roles as preacher, magistrate and missionary.

While he has used Simeon's sermon outlines slavishly, Marsden has, nevertheless, shown himself to be a man of Evangelical persuasion. His preaching style came to the critical attention of others.

---

[34] Our knowledge of this expectation of Governor Phillip comes from two letters from the Revd John Newton to the Revd Richard Johnson. The only extant copies of these letters are those published in James Bonwick, *Australia's First Preacher: The Revd Richard Johnson, First Chaplain of New South Wales* (London: Sampson Low, Marston & Co., 1898), pp 63-64, 67. The first of Newton's letters is dated 13 May 1787. The second is 24 June 1789. I am indebted to Craig Schwarze for this information.

[35] Grace Karskens, *The Colony: A History of Early Sydney* (Sydney: Allen & Unwin, 2009), p 12.

[36] Sermon 27:1

Nevertheless, it may well have set the standard and pattern by which the emerging Sydney clergy continued to proclaim the gospel.

Contrary to the perception of some, Marsden did not use the magistracy to shore up a diminishing influence as a clergyman.[37] As the years progressed beyond the 1820s, and the colony became less a penal colony than a land of free settlers seeking their fortune, Marsden's congregations grew significantly. Following his mentor, Simeon, Marsden believed simply that a well ordered society provided a secure place where the divine order of human society could be established. While Marsden may have earned a negative reputation as a magistrate in the colony, the thoughts and practices of Simeon nevertheless loom large over Marsden's ideas and behaviours. Marsden may well have also been heavily criticised for his involvement in the mission to New Zealand but in faithfully following his mentor he saw the proclamation of the gospel took precedence over restrictive roles of the Anglican clergyman. This was especially so where the conversion of many souls brought people into a well ordered society and church community.

It is without doubt that through the preaching and other activities of Samuel Marsden, Simeon of Cambridge has had a weighty influence on the development of Christian thought and practice in New South Wales.

---

[37] Yarwood has expressed this view. Cf. A T Yarwood, 'The Missionary Marsden: An Australian View', *New Zealand Journal of History*, 4.1 (1970), p 31.

4. Shaping the Anglican Church in Sydney, 1855-1882: Charles Simeon's Influence on Frederic Barker – *Grant Maple*

Frederic Barker, the second Anglican Bishop of Sydney and metropolitan of Australia, was born in March 1808. He matriculated as a pensioner to Jesus College, Cambridge on 27th January 1826. On his father's side, Barker was the son and grandson of Derbyshire clergymen who had benefitted from the patronage of successive Dukes of Devonshire, as Frederic and his eldest brother Anthony Auriol were to do. It appears that their father was a conscientious eighteenth century high church incumbent of the parish of Baslow on the edge of the Peak District. However it was their mother, Jane (neé Whyte of Liverpool) who exercised the strongest spiritual influence on her sons, particularly on Frederic.[1] Jane's grandmother had come from Presbyterian stock and her family had connections with Nonconformity and the Evangelicals of Lancashire and Yorkshire. Frederick Norman, nephew of the Duke of Rutland, recalled that in the long summer vacation of 1827 he and Frederic had gone hiking in the dales around Baslow. He said,

> On these occasions he [Frederic] always introduced subjects of profit, and he was to my mind as a schoolboy, a very holy and spiritual man. Everybody looked up to him – even his brother [Auriol], who was older than he, looked up to him – as living very much in the presence of GOD, and in near communion with him.[2]

We may conclude that Frederic Barker arrived at Cambridge a convinced Evangelical who practised the spiritual disciplines of what were termed at that time 'serious men'.

This study looks at the direct influence of Charles Simeon on Barker during his Cambridge undergraduate years (1826-1830). We then turn to the indirect influence of Simeon on Barker through the applied Simeonite Evangelicalism of his diocesan bishop, John Bird Sumner of Chester. The chapter explores how this influenced Barker's parish ministry and missionary endeavours at Upton, in Ireland and in Liverpool before considering how these influences were later used to fashion the shape of Sydney Diocese and the broader Australian Anglican Church.

---

[1] William Macquarie Cowper, *Episcopate of Frederic Barker, Bishop of Sydney and Metropolitan of Australia: A Memoir* (London: Hatchards, 1888), p 4.

[2] Cowper, *Episcopate of Frederic Barker*, p 4.

4.1. Charles Simeon's Direct Influence at Cambridge, 1827-1830

Among the friends that Barker made at Cambridge was Joseph Harden. Harden was three years ahead of Frederic in taking his degree but proceeded to ordination for the Diocese of Chester just a few months before Barker. Harden was a convinced Evangelical and one of 'Sim's men', being a founder of the Simeon-inspired Jesus Lane Sunday School and serving as its initial organising secretary.[3] There is no evidence of Barker having been involved in the Sunday School, which was mainly staffed by undergraduates from St. John's, Trinity and Queens' Colleges. However, Barker benefitted from Harden's influence which continued beyond Cambridge as the opportunities afforded. One such occasion was Frederic's invitation to Harden to preach at the fourth anniversary service of his induction into the parish of Edge Hill, Liverpool. On this happy occasion Harden brought and introduced his sister, Jane, to Barker. It was natural that they should ask Joseph to perform their marriage ceremony the following year.

Friendships such as this drew Barker into the circle of some sixty to eighty young men preparing for ordination who attended Charles Simeon's conversation parties in his King's College rooms on a Friday evening. An exact contemporary of Barker's, Abner Brown, recorded the content of discussions at these parties between 1827 and 1830.[4] Brown distinguished four types of gatherings that Simeon hosted: clerical meetings for those already ordained and in the early years of parish ministry; sermon classes for undergraduates which developed Simeon's philosophy of preaching derived from the French Huguenot Jean Claude, where students brought the fruit of their labours in exegeting a set passage of Scripture to which Simeon responded with his own insights;[5] the conversation parties which explored questions raised by

---

3   Charles Alfred Jones, *A History of the Jesus Lane Sunday School, Cambridge; With Short Biographical Notices of Some Deceased Teachers, and Lists of Superintendents, Teachers Etc. From Its Commencement* (London: William Macintosh, 1864), p 1. In this work Joseph Harden of St. John's is mentioned along with Messrs. Wright (the first Superintendent), Hiscock, Marsh and Clark of Queens' as the founders in response to a sermon by Charles Simeon. The list of Secretaries given on p 126 begins only in 1844. Barker may first have met Harden through William James Leach and Henry George Salter of Jesus College who were among some of the first teachers at Jesus Lane.

4   See Abner Brown, *Recollections of the Conversation Parties of the Revd Charles Simeon* (London: Hamilton, Adams, & Co., 1863).

5   These were set out in Simeon's progressive publication of sermon skeletons culminating in his *Horae Homileticae*, published in 21 volumes in 1835.

undergraduates, with occasional clerical visitors or overseas missionaries being present; and the more informal mixed social parties of Simeon's friends, former mentees and undergraduates. It is to the latter three that Barker was drawn.

Barker's prior commitment to an Evangelical faith, as well as his friendship with other disciples of Simeon, led him to see the value of the practical training which was based on the wisdom of Simeon's more than four decades of pastoral ministry. This was at a time when there was no pastoral theology or homiletic training available in the formal Cambridge curriculum, which was confined to mathematics with some philosophy and classics. The obligatory theology lectures for ordinands conducted by the Norrisian Professor, John Banks Hollingworth, were dry and focused on an exposition of Pearson's book on the Apostles' Creed.[6] Most students got by with attending as few divinity lectures as possible.

In considering Simeon's influence on the young Frederic Barker, one should not overlook Simeon's pulpit ministry. Undergraduates were obliged to attend their college chapel for an early perfunctory service after which they were free on a Sunday to attend Great St. Mary's to hear select preachers deliver the University Sermon, or to go to one of the numerous parish churches for the morning or evening sermon or the afternoon lecture. The mature Simeon in the last decade of his life had overcome much of the opposition of the early years so that his morning congregation at Holy Trinity was comprised of equal numbers of undergraduates and townspeople. Some Evangelicals did not like Simeon's style or his moderate Calvinism, preferring instead James Scholefield, Simeon's former curate and by 1825 Regius Professor of Greek and the incumbent Perpetual Curate of St. Michael's. Barker's Australian colleague Charles Perry, Bishop of Melbourne (1847-1876) was one such.[7] Another alternative was the Evangelical vicar of St. Giles and St. Peter's, the Jacksonian Professor of Natural Philosophy (1813-1837),

---

6   Most bishops required a certificate from Cambridge ordination candidates stating that they had attended twenty-five of Hollingworth's fifty lecture series – see David M Thompson, *Cambridge Theology in the Nineteenth Century: Enquiry, Controversy and Truth* (Aldershot: Ashgate, 2008), p 18. The new departure was the lectures of Herbert Marsh, Lady Margaret Professor, which for the first time were delivered in English at Great St. Mary's rather than the Divinity school, and which exposed students to the latest German higher criticism.

7   Arthur de Quetteville Robin, *Charles Perry, Bishop of Melbourne: The Challenges of a Colonial Episcopate, 1847-76* (Nedlands: University of Western Australia Press, 1967), pp 10-15.

William Farish. All three incumbents were like-minded in their support of Evangelical causes such as the British and Foreign Bible Society and the Church Missionary Society. It was Simeon, however, who had the greatest following and the most influential preaching ministry which was reinforced by his published sermon skeletons.

What might Barker have learnt from Simeon's conversation parties, sermon classes, preached sermons and informal social gatherings? Abner Brown identifies a number of aspects that are germane to Barker's subsequent ministry:

4.1.1. Ministerial character and duties

Simeon taught that the minister's example was more important than his preaching. He was against itinerancy as practised by Wesleyans. He insisted that duty to God involves application to your responsibilities while personal devotions and interests should be confined to one's leisure time.[8]

4.1.2. Theological position

Simeon held that when two opposite principles are found in the Bible, the truth does not lie, as some would have it, in Aristotle's golden mean but in steadily adopting both extremes. Thus he was a Clapham moderate Evangelical, not a premillennial Recordite Calvinist. He saw the latter as exaggerated, bordering on antinomianism and rationalism, whereas he was for moderation and faithfulness to the *Book of Common Prayer* and the Thirty-nine Articles, particularly the 'Grace' articles (nos. 9, 10, 11 & 17).[9]

4.1.3. The Scriptures

Simeon advocated studying the Bible diligently for oneself, allowing Scripture to be its own interpreter and only using commentaries to 'crack the bone' on difficult passages allowing the preacher to 'get at the marrow'. He recognised that Scripture often uses language 'that will not admit of literal interpretation'.[10]

4.1.4. Treating the text

Simeon identified four ways of treating the text: explication, which unfolds the text; observation, which draws out the substance with

---

8   Abner Brown, *Recollections*, p 36.
9   Abner Brown, *Recollections*, pp x, 11-12, 75-76.
10   Abner Brown, *Recollections*, pp 103-105, 210-212.

illustrations; propositions, which proves truths from the text; and application, which presses these on actions and habits.[11]

4.1.5.   Preaching

Simeon believed there was a threefold purpose of sermons: to instruct, to please and to affect the hearers. Instruction required solving the difficulties of the text, unfolding the mysteries of doctrine, penetrating the ways of divine wisdom, establishing truth and refuting error. By pleasing the hearers he meant comforting them and filling them with admiration for the ways of the Lord. Affecting them involved inflaming their souls with zeal to make them wish to practise piety, holiness and love.[12]

4.1.6.   Preaching style

Simeon advocated plainness and simplicity, staying with the text, using a conversational style and ensuring that the application was 'another turn of the screw'.[13]

4.1.7.   Hymns

Simeon advised that hymns should be used to reinforce the sermon.

4.1.8.   Ordination

Simeon advised ordination candidates to test whether the internal call they felt agreed with the external call recognised by those in authority in the church. He warned against thinking of ministry as a higher calling than lay vocations and was critical of parents who designated their children for ordained ministry before they reached an age when they were able to experience the double call.[14]

4.1.9.   Friction with older clergy

To avoid friction Simeon advised intending ordinands to concentrate on preaching the truth and visiting the people. They should only engage in extra-parochial religious societies with their Rector's approval.[15]

---

[11]   Abner Brown, *Recollections*, pp 184 f.
[12]   Preface to *Horae Homileticae*, I. p xxi.
[13]   Abner Brown, *Recollections*, p 197.
[14]   Abner Brown, *Recollections*, pp 207 f.
[15]   Abner Brown, *Recollections*, p 213.

4.1.10. Pastoral visiting

Simeon held that it was best to speak face to face rather than conveying things in writing. Young clergy should beware of overwork. The remedy was to nominate elders, laymen and women to visit the sick, pray with them and read the Scriptures to them. The minister could then meet with lay people to discover the greatest needs for him to address.[16]

4.1.11. Involvement in Christian societies

Simeon was an early supporter of the Cambridge auxiliary of the British and Foreign Bible Society (from 1811) despite criticism from High Church supporters of the Society for the Promotion of Christian Knowledge. He supported the Society for Missions in Africa and the East (from 1799, later known as the Church Missionary Society), despite criticisms from the supporters of the Society for the Propagation of the Gospel. Simeon also supported the London Society for Promoting Christianity among the Jews (from 1815). He justified this on the basis that a number of the bishops gave their support to these new societies as well as to the longer-standing SPCK and SPG.[17]

4.1.12. Clerical societies

Simeon had connections with the Clapham sect, the Yorkshire Evangelicals, the Elland and Bristol clerical societies and supported others who formed such Evangelical societies in Derbyshire and the north-west.[18]

4.1.13. Sunday schools

Simeon stimulated undergraduates to consider the needs of the Cambridge poor in forming the Jesus Lane Sunday School in Barnwell, a poorer area of Cambridge. He saw this as a way of bringing the gospel to families who otherwise were outside the reach of the established church.[19]

---

[16] Abner Brown, *Recollections*, pp 165 f, 195.

[17] Abner Brown, *Recollections*, pp 335f.

[18] Arthur Pollard, 'The Influence and Significance of Simeon's Work', in *Charles Simeon (1759-1836): Essays Written in Commemoration of His Bi-Centenary by Members of the Evangelical Fellowship for Theological Literature* (London: SPCK, 1959), p 180.

[19] Jones, *A History of the Jesus Lane Sunday School*, p 1.

4.1.14. *Working holidays*

Simeon travelled to Scotland in 1796, 1798 and 1819, and to Ireland in 1822 where he preached and laboured 'in the cause of godliness and religion'.[20]

As will be subsequently shown, Frederic Barker's parish ministry and episcopal leadership displayed plentiful evidence of Simeon's direct influence.

4.2. *Charles Simeon's Indirect Influence through Fellow Evangelicals*

Frederic Barker was ordained for ministry in the Diocese of Chester. This diocese was remarkable in the early part of the nineteenth century for the massive growth of the industrial towns of Lancashire and their ports. Such growth provided opportunities for ministry as new churches were established. Reform of the diocese had begun under Bishop Charles Blomfield (1824-1828) before his translation to London. It was continued by the Evangelical Bishop John Bird Sumner from 1828 until his translation to the archbishopric of Canterbury in 1848. Sumner licensed a significant number of Evangelical clergy as parishes became vacant. Barker's early ministry was at Upton on the Wirral Peninsula across the Mersey, followed by nineteen years at Edge Hill, Liverpool.

Simeon's indirect influence was conveyed in a number of ways:

4.2.1. *Personal friendships*

Mention has already been made of Joseph Harden who served at Hawkshead in Yorkshire. Another close friend was Charles Lawrence who ministered at St. Luke's, Liverpool.[21] Barker and Lawrence worked with the more militant Irish Evangelical, Hugh MacNeile, minister of St. Jude's on a number of Evangelical committees.

---

[20] Abner Brown, *Recollections*, p 4.
[21] Cowper, *Episcopate of Frederic Barker*, p 22. Although Lawrence was an Oxford graduate, he shared many of the concerns that Simeon had imbued in his disciples. The closeness of their relationship can be measured by the fact that Charles Lawrence named his eldest son 'William Frederic' (who went on to be Conservative MP for Liverpool Abercrombie from 1885-1906).

4.2.2. Liverpool clerical meetings

At least thirteen other Liverpool clergy were Evangelicals. These men may have differed in outlook but they had a commitment to the gospel and to supporting their bishop's vision for the diocese. Of these Hugh MacNeile was a premillennial Recordite; Thomas Tattershall (St. Augustine's), chair of the Liverpool Protestant Association, was a scholarly Simeonite moderate; Fielding Ould (Christ Church), attacked Unitarianism, the Liverpool Corporation's plans for a non-religious liberal education and premillennial views on the restoration of Jews to Palestine; John Jones (St. Andrew's), was a protégé of Charles Simeon and of the Gladstone family, later becoming Archdeacon of Liverpool; William Withers Ewbank (St. George's), was a controversialist and commentary writer; Henry Carpenter (St. Michael's) was also a moderate in the Simeon mould, whose son became bishop of Ripon; and Charles Lawrence was sympathetic to Simeon's ideals. In combined activities Simeon's thoughtful approach to issues was never far from the surface. Mention should also be made of John Tyrrel Baylee, an Irish Evangelical who in 1840 became the first incumbent of Holy Trinity Church, Birkenhead and who went on to become the first Principal of St. Aidan's College.

4.2.3. Evangelical society membership

Frederic Barker along with most of the other Evangelicals was a member of the local auxiliaries of the Irish Home Mission; the British and Foreign Bible Society; the Church Missionary Society; and the Liverpool Scripture Readers' Society.[22] These were either societies that Simeon himself was directly involved with, both financially and as guest preacher or speaker, or were closely akin to similar groups to which Simeon gave unconditional support.[23]

4.2.4. Bishop John Bird Sumner

The strongest transmission and application of Simeon's ideals is to be found in the work of Barker's diocesan bishop. In forging a reform program for Chester diocese Sumner blended Simeon's approach to pastoral ministry with Thomas Chalmers' recent work at the Tron

---

[22] Barker, MacNeile and Lawrence worked together to support *la famille-Évangélique* at La Force in France in its work amongst afflicted and desolate young girls – see Cowper, *Episcopate of Frederic Barker*, p 22.

[23] Abner Brown, *Recollections*, p 335 f.

Church in Glasgow. Sumner's biographer identified four key aspects of this program:[24] the provision of increased church accommodation, especially for the poor, which involved the establishment in 1834 of the Chester Diocesan Church Building Society; the encouragement and support of an active body of clergy especially by augmenting their numbers through the establishment in 1846 of St. Aidan's College, Birkenhead, the diocesan training college for non-graduate ordinands;[25] the advocacy of lay visitors and lay helpers in each parish and the establishment in 1832 of the Lancashire Visiting Society and in 1838 of the Cheshire Visiting Society; and the promotion of education through church schools and Sunday schools.[26] The latter included the founding in 1839 of Chester College for the training of teachers for church schools.[27] Sumner's triennial visitation charges carried this forward.[28] Each of these initiatives was copied by Frederic Barker in Sydney.

4.3. Frederic Barker's Parish Ministry: Upton, Ireland, Edge Hill and Baslow

The application of Simeon's ideas can be seen in Barker's ministries between 1831 and 1854.

4.3.1. Upton (1831-1834)

Frederic Barker was made deacon on 10th April 1831 and was appointed as Stipendiary Curate to Upton (also known as Overchurch) in the Diocese of Chester.[29] This meant that he was placed in sole charge of this small rural parish without the usual guidance of a senior parish clergyman. Proximity to Birkenhead and Liverpool meant frequent contact with likeminded people in Liverpool, from whose experience he could draw. He developed a particular interest in the Irish Mission,

---

24 Nigel Scotland, *The Life and Work of John Bird Sumner, Evangelical Archbishop* (Leominster: Gracewing, 1995), pp 48 ff.

25 See F B Heiser, *The Story of Saint Aiden's College Birkenhead, 1847-1947* (Chester: Phillipson & Goulder, 1950), pp 9 ff.

26 The diocesan Chancellor, the Revd Henry Raikes, was nephew of Robert Raikes of Gloucester, who is credited with starting the Sunday school movement.

27 See John L Bradbury, *Chester College and the Training of Teachers, 1839-1975* (Chester: Governors of Chester College, 1975), pp 23-24.

28 See John Bird Sumner, *A Charge Delivered to the Clergy of the Diocese of Chester at the Primary Visitation in August and September 1829* (London: Hatchard and Son, 1829). And subsequent triennia.

29 After being priested in April 1832 he was made Perpetual Curate.

where he served as itinerant missioner and then supervisor during a period of leave from Upton in 1834.

Since no records remain of his time at Upton and the history of the church is silent about the incumbents before 1847,[30] one can only imagine Frederic Barker conscientiously applying what he had learnt from his father and from Charles Simeon in this small rural parish while seeking to implement the mission objectives of his bishop. That he was judicious and proved himself worthy of this responsibility is borne out by the fact that he soon attracted notice of others and was offered larger responsibilities as a mission supervisor while in Ireland and the possibility of larger Irish and English parishes.[31] It was while he was in Ireland that he received the offer of St. Mary's Edge Hill in Liverpool, which he accepted.

4.3.2. Edge Hill (1835-1854)

This was a mixed parish on the edge of Liverpool which was undergoing rapid expansion, lying as it did at the western terminus of the Liverpool–Manchester railway which had opened on 15th September 1830. Established wealthy merchant families, tradespeople and a growing number of poor labourers now constituted its membership. Barker's ministry there followed lines advocated by Simeon.

From its foundation in 1813 the church had catered primarily for the affluent who lived in this semi-rural elevated part of the town. In meeting the changing demographic, Barker seized the opportunity to address the needs of the poor by conducting an evening service in the parish schoolroom, where seating was free and the service was simplified and shortened using extempore prayer and a plain address. As this expanded, he supported the establishment of nearby St. Clement's, Windsor and, within his own parish, set about raising £100 per week by appealing to five or six different wealthier parishioners each week to build St. Stephen the Martyr church to cater for the working families. It was opened without debt and was well attended by the poor who 'flocked to it in great numbers.' Another daughter church was in the planning stage when he resigned in 1854 to succeed his elder brother and father at Baslow. As part of his strategy to

---

30 Robert A Pullen and Kenneth J Burnley, *Set Upon a Hill: The Story of St. Mary's Church and Parish Upton, Wirral* (Upton: St Mary's Parish Church, 1993), p 13.

31 Barker was offered Stoney Middleton in Derbyshire and Rathkeale in County Limerick – see Cowper, *Episcopate of Frederic Barker*, p 9.

reach the unchurched, Barker supported and engaged in open air preaching as the first step in planning another church to accommodate those who responded.[32]

His preaching followed the Simeon model of expounding the Scriptures. He covered whole books sequentially in his 'lectures' as well as preaching from the Gospel and Epistle for the day. The prophetic books formed the substance of his Lenten addresses. He is recorded as covering the Pentateuch, James, Acts, and Job among others. One of his parishioners recalled that under his guidance many loved to search the Scriptures for themselves.[33] Four of his five extant sermons were against the errors of Roman Catholicism and such tendencies in the Church of England.[34] These reveal that Barker was not averse to contending for what he saw to be the truth in current controversies in a town with a large immigrant Irish Roman Catholic population.

His church services were notable for their 'heartfelt solemnity'. A friend commented that 'his ministry owed its power most of all to his own waiting upon God, and the way in which he asked for and depended upon God's blessing on his preaching.'[35] His confirmation preparation was thorough and his confirmees were channelled afterwards into Bible classes. He was admired for his tender administration to the sick and the aged.[36]

Barker was firmly committed to education. He warmly promoted the parish school which had an average attendance of 350 pupils. It used the Bell system of a master and pupil-teachers. He supported the National Society for the Education of the Poor in the Principles of the Established Church in establishing further schools in Liverpool. Along with other Evangelicals he appears to have stood against the Liverpool Corporation's attempts to establish non-religious liberal education. St. Mary's parish also had a thriving Sunday School, a number of its

---

[32]   Cowper, *Episcopate of Frederic Barker*, pp 19f.

[33]   Cowper, *Episcopate of Frederic Barker*, p 24.

[34]   The earliest, 'The supposed sacrament of penance' (9th December 1835), was one of a series of ten sermons preached in 1835-1836 by Evangelical Liverpool clergy in response to Roman Catholic emancipation and the beginnings of the Tractarian Movement within the Church of England. Another, 'On the rise of errors in the Church of Rome' dates from 1838. Two more were preached in January 1851: 'The idolatrous worship of the Church of Rome' and 'Not peace but a sword or a plea for controversy'. The remaining sermon from the 29 December 1844 was on 'The incarnation of the Son of God.'

[35]   Cowper, *Episcopate of Frederic Barker*, p 25.

[36]   Cowper, *Episcopate of Frederic Barker*, p 25.

teachers subsequently entering the ministry, two of whom joined Barker in Sydney. The parish was divided into districts and lay visitors were appointed to each on the Simeon model.[37]

Barker had a leading role with four other Evangelical clergy in establishing the Liverpool Scripture Readers' Society whose object was to promote the diffusion of Scriptural knowledge throughout the city and its neighbourhood. It employed Scripture readers, licensed by the bishop and under the direction of clergy to arrange sermons, lectures and classes for instruction. Barker revealed his ability to unite people of differing views in support of this society. He continued to support the Irish Mission and he held quarterly meetings in his school hall of a Church Missionary Society auxiliary. Barker was also a strong supporter of the interdenominational British and Foreign Bible Society and the County Refuge founded by the Quaker Elizabeth Fry for the reformation of females.[38]

Of great significance was Barker's personal influence and power to draw men around him. These included E J Nixon who accompanied Barker to Australia, V W Ryan who was consecrated with Barker on St Andrew's Day 1854 as Bishop of Mauritius, and J S Howson who was second master at the Collegiate Institution but was encouraged by Barker to seek ordination. A contemporary observed that he formed around him 'a band of clergy of unusual ability, in some ways no doubt of ability superior to his own.'[39]

4.3.3. Baslow (1854)

The death of his eldest brother Anthony Auriol at the age of fifty-three while incumbent of Baslow parish, saw the patron, the Duke of Devonshire, offering the parish to Frederic. Recurring bouts of ill health that necessitated leave from Edge Hill parish to travel to warmer climates led Frederic to accept the living. Just after moving back to Baslow the invitation came from his former diocesan and now Archbishop of Canterbury, J B Sumner, to lead the Australian church as bishop of Sydney and Metropolitan of Australia.

---

[37] Cowper, *Episcopate of Frederic Barker*, p 21. The two who accompanied him to Sydney were Edward Synge and Walter Richardson.

[38] Cowper, *Episcopate of Frederic Barker*, p 22.

[39] Cowper, *Episcopate of Frederic Barker*, p 21.

4.4. Barker's Leadership of Sydney Diocese

On his arrival in Sydney on 25th May 1855 Barker was confronted with an extensive diocese that covered three quarters of the land area of New South Wales.[40] The discovery of gold in 1851 had led to a rapid expansion of a dispersed population. The church had languished during the hiatus between the departure (and subsequent death) of his predecessor, Bishop William Grant Broughton, on 16th August 1852 and Barker's arrival thirty three months later.

He discovered that most of the larger city parishes were staffed by High Churchmen, some with strong Tractarian sympathies. The diocese had been dutifully administered by the elderly Archdeacon William Cowper, an Evangelical. Barker found a lack of institutions, church accommodation and clergy to minister to the burgeoning population. He also had experienced difficulty in recruiting sufficient clergy to accompany him to Australia. To add to the burden, the newly-formed University of Sydney was a secular foundation and the bishop was given a very limited role in the Anglican residential St. Paul's College.

Barker's response was to adopt many of the elements of Sumner's applied Simeonite model. His immediate priority was to establish a new theological college to augment the number of clergy. To do this he took advantage of the legacy left by Thomas Moore. From this emerged Moore College which was designed on the model of St. Aidan's Birkenhead and led by one of Barker's English Evangelical friends, William Hodgson. The college was to prove beneficial for the Australian church by providing ordinands for many dioceses in the second half of the nineteenth century.[41]

Barker's next step was to form a diocesan Church Society to raise funds to support church extension. He brought William Macquarie Cowper who had been instrumental in setting up a similar society in

---

[40] Sydney Diocese in 1855 included the dioceses of Bathurst, Canberra-Goulburn and Riverina. The other NSW diocese at that time was Newcastle which included the present dioceses of Armidale and Grafton.

[41] For a detailed description of the founding and operations of Moore College and lists of its graduates, see Marcus L Loane, *A Centenary History of Moore Theological College* (Sydney: Angus and Robertson, 1955).

Newcastle Diocese to Sydney to set about this task.[42] The twin objects of the society were to raise finance for new church buildings and to supplement the stipends of clergy in parishes that were not self-sufficient, especially needful after the withdrawal of state aid to churches by the NSW government in 1862.

Barker took particular trouble over the pastoral care of clergy, especially the young and vulnerable. Like Sumner, he attempted through his visitation addresses to create a diocesan culture by inspiring the clergy to embrace a larger vision of mission. Unlike his predecessor, he understood the concerns of the Irish clergy and was able to harness their energies for the development of the parishes and diocese. Barker set up rural deaneries headed by senior clergy to mentor younger clergy who were often placed in sole charge after a minimal time as an assistant curate. Conscious of the needs of clergy, he set the goal of £300 as the minimum stipend for incumbents, he instituted a superannuation fund to provide for them in retirement, and a clergy widow and orphans' fund to protect their families from destitution. He supported lay involvement at parish, diocesan and inter-diocesan levels. He advocated lay visitation in parishes along the lines of Simeon and Sumner. The Chester model was used to establish a Lay Readers' Institute in 1875 to supplement the work of overstretched clergy. From 1869 a system was established for parish representatives to participate in making a nomination to the bishop of the next incumbent for a parish.[43]

Barker's own preaching and what he looked for in his clergy was according to Simeon's dictum that a sermon was 'an exhaustive treatise on a single text practically applied.' Where his preaching differed from a number of his clergy was in his emphasis on, and their lack of focus regarding, redemption through Christ's atoning death on the cross. Typical of many of their generation, all too many of them preached moral reformation.[44]

---

[42] See D G Anderson, 'The Bishop's Society, 1856-1958: A History of the Sydney Anglican Home Mission Society' (unpublished Ph.D. Thesis, University of Wollongong, 1990).

[43] This provided an alternate way to that of the English patronage system to ensure that suitable clergy were appointed to parishes. It was further democratised in 1875 – see Grant S Maple, 'Evangelical Anglicanism – Dominant, Defensive or in Decline? A Study of Church Life and Organisation in the Diocese of Sydney during the Episcopate of Frederic Barker, 1855-1882' (unpublished M.A. Hons. Thesis, Macquarie University, 1992), pp 78 ff.

[44] Maple, 'Evangelical Anglicanism', p 132.

Education was another challenge that Barker dealt with. He took advantage of the dual system established in NSW in 1848 to develop parish schools. By 1861 there were 107 in the diocese. Soon after their arrival Jane Barker brought to her husband's attention the need for a school to educate clergy daughters. Barker secured the funds and five acres of land at Waverley to establish in 1856 St Catherine's, the first girls' school in Australia. It was modelled on Casterton School in Westmorland.[45]

In 1856 Barker also created a position of inspector of schools to improve the standard of teaching and learning. The following year he established the Church of England Training School for Teachers on the model of Chester College. He encouraged the clergy to enrol all Anglican children in these schools. With the passage of the 1866 Public Schools Act by the NSW government, which brought all state-aided schools under the control of the Council of Education, Barker gained amendments which gave clergy the right to enter all Council schools to provide religious instruction. In the lead up to the subsequent 1880 Public Instruction Act, Barker unsuccessfully fought to maintain the position of church schools. When it was apparent that many of his laity and clergy had deserted his concept of the church school being the focus of evangelism and instruction in Christian living in favour of non-denominational state schools offering liberal secular instruction, Barker fought for the continued right of entry in these schools for religious instruction. During these years there was dramatic growth in Anglican Sunday Schools with attendances trebling between 1867 and 1880.[46]

Like Simeon, Barker was keen to advance the cause of the local auxiliaries of the British and Foreign Bible Society and the Church Missionary Society. He supported the non-denominational Sydney City Mission in its work among the poor but was reluctant to be involved in any religious society, such as Temperance organisations, which were likely to cause divisions among Anglicans. Again like Simeon he did not permit himself or his clergy to share pulpits with other

---

[45] Casterton School had been founded in 1823 at Cowan Bridge by another of Simeon's disciples, the Revd William Carus Wilson. After being moved to Casterton, it was the school attended by the three daughters of another Evangelical, the Revd Patrick Brontë.

[46] See P D Davis, 'Bishop Barker and Education' (unpublished M.Ed Thesis, University of Sydney, 1963).

denominations.47 Barker supported and gained some assistance from the SPCK and SPG and fostered interest in the Melanesian Mission, particularly after the martyrdom of Bishop J C Patteson in 1871. He also fostered the establishment of a Home Visiting and Relief Society in 1862 to provide for the necessitous, and a District Visitors Association with branches in many parishes. Anglican clergy and church members were at the forefront in providing relief during the 1864 floods on the Hawkesbury and Shoalhaven rivers and during the 1869 drought in western parts of the colony.

Barker's careful development of synodical self-government, his responses to rationalism and ritualism, his support for missions, his development of a diocesan response to social problems, and his respect for opponents all bore the marks of his mentors, Charles Simeon and John Bird Sumner.48 His disappointment at the failure of Evangelical clergy and laity to see what was at stake in the major issues of public elementary education, the relation of the church to the university, divorce law reform, declining Lord's Day observance, and other issues stemmed from his broader appreciation of the theological issues at stake.

As Metropolitan bishop of the Church of England in Australia, Barker provided leadership in a number of significant ways. He worked diligently for the subdivision of the diocese by canvassing for an endowment (in each case of £10,000) and the securing of capable Evangelical bishops for Goulburn and Bathurst dioceses in the persons of Mesac Thomas (1863) and Samuel Edward Marsden (1870). In 1877 he obtained the appointment of George Henry Stanton as bishop of North Queensland.

His careful work in negotiating with the NSW Parliament the passage of the 1866 Act for the management of church property opened the way for diocesan and provincial synods comprised of three houses – bishops, clergy and lay people. Building on the work of his predecessor, Barker overcame constitutional and theological differences in negotiating with his fellow bishops the first General Synod for the church in Australia (1872).

---

47 Simeon made an exception, which Barker did not, of being prepared to preach in Presbyterian pulpits when in Scotland on the grounds that it was the established church of Scotland.

48 Scotland, *The Life and Work of John Bird Sumner*, pp 67 ff.

One of the most significant contributions to the life of the broader church was the number of clergy trained at Moore College who served in other dioceses – sixty ordinands for Melbourne diocese, twenty for Bathurst, seven each for Goulburn and North Queensland and five for Ballarat.[49]

4.5. *Barker's Enduring Influence on the Character of the Diocese.*

Through the episcopal leadership of Frederic Barker, Charles Simeon influenced the Anglican church in Sydney Diocese and beyond. Barker saw the importance of clergy being trained to understand and exegete the Bible, focusing on the saving work of Christ and applying its teaching to the lives of the people. Barker's crowning achievement was his founding of Moore College with its emphasis on biblical studies and conservative Evangelical theology.

Along with this was a determination not to let minor issues and the fashions of the day deflect the church from its mission to Australian society. Barker resisted secularism and the various forms of ritualism and rationalism that gripped other parts of the church and society.

Barker established a culture of mission in the diocese. He was concerned about ministry to Aboriginal people groups, to Chinese immigrants on the gold fields, to the Pacific island peoples as well as to the largely overlooked working class families within the diocese. The outstanding success story was the ministry of St. Barnabas parish in Broadway under the layman Thomas Smith, who was later ordained. Church people were encouraged to support the British and Foreign Bible Society, the Church Missionary Society and the Sydney City Mission.

Lay people were given an active role in ministry through the use of lay readers to supplement ordained ministry, through district visiting societies in parishes, through teaching Sunday school, through the work of the Church Society and other institutions designed to advance the work of the church. They were also given an equal voice to the clergy in the diocesan, provincial and general synods.

Barker's strong commitment to school education saw the early establishment of St. Catherine's School, the reformation of The King's School, the expansion of parish schools and the establishment of a

---

49 Loane, *A Centenary History*, pp 180-183.

training college for teachers. Standards were to be raised by the appointment of an inspector of schools. Much of this work was undermined by the cessation of state aid and the assumption of responsibility by government in 1880 for compulsory elementary education. Barker was able to negotiate right of access to public schools for the clergy for religious instruction, an enduring feature of education in NSW.

Concern for the poor and underprivileged was never far from Barker's thoughts. To this end he established a number of funds and agencies to have the dual function of meeting physical needs and at the same time bringing the gospel into the lives of those on the fringes of society.

Finally, in his appointment of clergy to senior positions in the diocese and in his selection of bishops in new dioceses he sought out capable Evangelicals for preferment. The provision of well-trained Evangelical clergy from Moore College helped during Barker's lifetime to sustain the Evangelical mission of the church in the diocese and beyond.

5. From King's College to Kingsford: Charles Simeon's Enduring Influence on Australian University Ministry – *Edward Loane*

The earlier chapters of this book have begun to demonstrate the tremendous influence Charles Simeon had on Christianity in Australia. Particularly in the first hundred years of European occupation, leaders who were personally mentored by Simeon held highly significant leadership roles within the churches of the colony. In this chapter I propose to step back from his personal influence and examine, rather more broadly, the influence of Simeon on Evangelical university ministry in Australia. In his recent biography of Simeon, Derek Prime says, 'Perhaps the most exciting and fascinating illustration of Simeon's influence is Evangelical witness in the world's universities.'[1] This chapter will examine the ministry to university students in Cambridge all those years ago and demonstrate its enduring influence in Australian universities with particular reference to Phillip Jensen's ministry at The University of New South Wales.

Simeon's continued significance to university ministry in Australia may, at first, appear to be somewhat tenuous. After all, when Simeon was converted as a student in 1779, the American War of Independence raged on and it was not until 1783 that Australia was even suggested as an alternative penal colony.[2] As an undergraduate, Simeon claimed that he never met a likeminded Evangelical.[3] It was not until he was made vicar of Holy Trinity in 1782, still five years before the First Fleet departed, that he began a ministry to students. Certainly by the time he died in 1836, the settlement in Sydney was established, but the church in Australia had only enthroned its first bishop three months earlier and there were definitely no universities – and there would not be any

---

[1] Derek Prime, *Charles Simeon: An Ordinary Pastor of Extraordinary Influence*, History Today (Leominster: Day One, 2011), p 239.

[2] This was first suggested by Admiral Sir George Young, whose descendants would in due course make significant contributions to Christianity in Sydney, notably in the establishment of the Katoomba Christian Convention and the C.M.S. Summer School. Stuart Braga and Patricia Braga, *All His Benefits: Young and Deck Families* (Self Published, 2013), p 6-9. Cf. Stuart Braga, *A Century Preaching Christ: Katoomba Christian Convention, 1903-2003* (Sydney: KCC, 2003).

[3] Hugh Evans Hopkins, *Charles Simeon of Cambridge* (Eugene, Oregon: Wipf & Stock, 1977), p 29.

universities in Australia for another fifteen years.[4] This chronological disparity between Simeon and Australian university ministries begs the question of how tenable the claim is that he significantly influenced Evangelical university ministry in Australia – a ministry which now includes over fifty university campuses across the country.

The dissimilarities between Cambridge in Simeon's day and contemporary Australian universities, however, extend much further than just time and place. Cambridge in the early nineteenth century was virtually a Church of England seminary with more than half of graduates becoming clergymen.[5] The university was a confessional institution where 'Non-Anglicans were *de facto* excluded' because students had to sign the Thirty-Nine Articles in order to graduate.[6] While that university underwent 'a complete transformation' into a modern secular institution in the latter half of the nineteenth century,[7] Australian universities, such as The University of Sydney and The University of New South Wales, were strictly founded upon secular ideology.[8]

Another major dissimilarity was the size and cultural diversity of the universities. In Simeon's day Cambridge was quite small and Simeon's

---

4   Simeon died on 13 November 1836. Bishop Broughton was enthroned on 5 June 1836 and Sydney University was founded in 1851.

5   Peter Searby states, 'During the 120 years considered in this volume Cambridge was an Anglican seminary.' This was a declining percentage over this period, however, as between 1752 and 1769 more than three quarters (76%) of Cambridge graduates became clergymen, but by 1870-1886 that percentage had reduced to 38%. Nevertheless, it was still the most popular graduate profession. Peter Searby, *A History of the University of Cambridge: Volume 3, 1750-1870* (Cambridge: Cambridge University Press, 1997), p 76.

6   Michael Hofstetter, *The Romantic Idea of a University: England and Germany, 1770-1850* (Basingstoke: Palgrave, 2001), p 3. This changed over the course of the century and religious tests were abolished so students were no longer forced to sign the 39 Articles to receive their degree and by 1877, fellowships and college headships were no longer bound to holy orders. Timothy Gouldstone, *The Rise and Decline of Anglican Idealism in the Nineteenth Century* (Palgrave MacMillan, 2005), p xiii.

7   Vivian Green, *Religion at Oxford and Cambridge* (London: SCM, 1964), p 297.

8   When Sydney University was founded, William Charles Wentworth was adamant that it be an institution 'merely for secular education' claiming 'This principle was absolutely indispensable; if they once introduce the principle of sectarian interference, all government of such an institution was at an end, because if any one sect asserted its supremacy, all other sects would retire from it, and thus be virtually excluded from participation in its benefits' cited in, Clifford Turney, Ursula Bygott and Peter Chippendale, *Australia's First: A History of the University of Sydney Volume 1, 1850-1939* (Sydney: Hale & Iremonger, 1991), p 43.

College, King's, was the smallest and most exclusive of them all. In 1795 there were only 736 undergraduates in the university and just twelve in King's.[9] Simeon himself matriculated with only two other freshmen, and the college, ever since its foundation, had only accepted students from Eton.[10] It was a college of prestige and privilege. For example, students at King's had the unique privilege of being allowed to take their degrees without any examinations and could take a fellowship automatically after three years residence.[11] Furthermore, all university students were required to reside in college accommodation. Contrast that university experience with the more than 50,000 students currently at The University of New South Wales of which more than one quarter are international students and only two percent reside at the university.[12] A basic comparison of the two spheres would suggest that such great differences mitigate against a case for Simeon's enduring influence. Yet, we will see that despite such a great gulf in the culture, demography and ideology, Simeon's example remains an encouragement for contemporary Australian university ministry.

5.1. Simeon's University Ministry

In the months before taking up the incumbency of Holy Trinity in 1782, Simeon made six trips to visit Revd Henry Venn at Yelling, a village twelve miles west of Cambridge. Venn was an elder statesman of the Evangelical movement and was very pleased with the potential good Simeon could do in the university town. On 9 October 1782 he wrote that his guest was 'calculated for great usefulness', was 'full of faith and love' and flamed with zeal.[13] The Bishop of Ely, a friend of Simeon's father, provided him with the platform in which to conduct his ministry, despite much opposition from the wardens and parishioners of Holy Trinity.[14] Simeon had often walked past the church and thought to himself 'How I should rejoice if God were to give me that church, that I might preach the Gospel there, and be a herald for him in the midst of

---

9   Searby, *A History of the University of Cambridge*, p 11.

10 Hopkins, *Charles Simeon of Cambridge*, p 10 f/n.

11 Hopkins, *Charles Simeon of Cambridge*, p 19.

12 Figures found at http://myuniversity.gov.au/University-of-New-South-Wales/3013#!uni-stats/tables and http://www.rc.unsw.edu.au/colleges/unsw-colleges accessed 11 May 2015.

13 9 October 1782 – Henry Venn, *The Life and a Selection from the Letters of the Late Revd Henry Venn*, ed. by John Venn, 6th edn (London, 1855), p 263.

14 John Pollock, *A Cambridge Movement* (London: John Murray, 1953), p 3

the University'.[15] It was not long, however, for him to be making an impression on the university. In 1786 Venn wrote in a letter to Revd Rowland Hill 'Mr Simeon's light shines brighter and brighter. He is highly esteemed, and exceedingly despised; almost adored by some; by others abhorred. O what numbers, if the Lord will, shall come out of Cambridge in a few years, to proclaim glad tidings!'[16] It had not taken long for Simeon to be counted a significant presence in the university, as both the support and opposition testified. But what did the shape of his ministry to students look like?

First, we must highlight Simeon's emphasis on expository preaching. This became the foundation of his ministry and was a legacy that he left for Evangelicals in the years to come. Simeon, like other clergymen of his day, would not have received any training in preaching prior to ordination.[17] Yet, in his ministry he came to the firm conclusion that it was the systematic preaching of Scripture that was the heart of Christian ministry. He said,

> Be not afraid of speaking all that God has spoken in his word, or of giving to every word of his the measure of weight and emphasis and preponderance, that it has in the inspired writings. The instant that you are afraid or averse to do this, you stand self-condemned, as sitting in judgment upon him, from whom every word has been inspired for the good of the Church.[18]

With this conviction in mind, Simeon set about to address the problem of preaching by instigating sermon classes for students. These classes began in 1792 and continued for forty years. They were held on Sundays after church for about fifteen to twenty undergraduates.[19] They generally involved Simeon selecting a text for students to prepare a sermon in skeleton form and then as they explained it to him, he would comment

---

[15] Carus, *Memoirs of the Life*, p 37.

[16] Edwin Sidney, *The Life of the Revd Rowland Hill* (London: Baldwin & Cradock, 1834), p 158.

[17] Prime, *Charles Simeon*, p 67. C.f. George Peacock's comment, 'At least one-half the students in the university are designed for the church, and no provision (the lectures of the Norrisian professor alone excepted) is made for their professional education; this is a deficiency in our academical system'. George Peacock, *Observations on the Statutes of the University of Cambridge* (London, 1841), p 168.

[18] Carus, *Memoirs of the Life*, pp 511-12.

[19] Kenneth Hylson-Smith, *Evangelicals in the Church of England: 1734-1984* (Edinburgh: T & T Clark, 1988), p 74.

on how he thought it could be improved.[20] These classes were so influential that at the turn of the next century George Balleine would claim that they were the place where 'most of the Evangelical preachers of the next generation were trained'.[21]

In a similar way, Simeon attempted to fill the lacuna of theological education within the university. For an example of how seriously the authorities took the teaching of doctrine, in 1802 neither the Regus Professor of Divinity nor the Lady Margaret Professor of Divinity gave a single lecture.[22] Simeon sought to address this dereliction by conducting his own Conversation Parties. Although initially reluctant due to the Conventicles Act, in 1813 he began to invite groups of students to his rooms at King's on Friday evenings to discuss theology.[23] The students would crowd in and then, with the windows shut tight for fear of fresh air, questions would be asked and Simeon would teach them.[24] These parties provided theological education that was probably unparalleled in the country.[25] Indeed, Max Warren argues that they were a unique initiative that 'anticipated the later development of Theological Colleges'.[26]

As Venn noted early on in Simeon's ministry, the uncompromising Evangelical witness in the university entailed severe opposition. It was not uncommon for rowdy groups of undergraduates to try and break up his services.[27] But Simeon, with a tenacity that is rarely seen, remained focused on his calling for fifty-four years and ultimately saw much fruit from his labour. His own assessment of the task he had undertaken was absolutely foundational for his ability to persist through such great difficulties. Indeed, Ford Brown argued that very few people succeed in achieving such a 'rigorous conception of what they ought to do' as Simeon did.[28] Simeon once claimed, 'I look on my position here as the highest and most important in the kingdom, nor would I exchange it for

---

20 Prime, *Charles Simeon*, p 68.
21 Balleine, *History of the Evangelical Party*, p 102.
22 Hopkins, *Charles Simeon of Cambridge*, p 20.
23 Max Warren, *Charles Simeon* (London: Church Book Room, 1959), p 7, Hylson-Smith, *Evangelicals in the Church of England*, p 74.
24 Pollock, *A Cambridge Movement*, p 5.
25 Hylson-Smith, *Evangelicals in the Church of England*, p 74.
26 Warren, *Charles Simeon*, p 22.
27 Steer, *Church on Fire*, p 166.
28 Ford Brown, *Fathers of the Victorians: The Age of Wilberforce* (Cambridge: Cambridge University Press, 1961), p 292.

any other'.[29] When discussing the option of marriage and the entailing necessity of surrendering his fellowship, Simeon was completely frank. He said, 'the singular way in which I have been called to my present post, and its almost incalculable importance, forbid the thought of my now leaving it: therefore I think I shall never marry'.[30] There was no doubt in Simeon's mind of the strategic importance of his university ministry and his calling to it. Armed with this assurance, all opposition was patiently endured and the cumulative impact of his work was multiplied over the long term.

One of the great joys of over half a century's labour for Simeon was to reflect on the change that had taken place in that time. In 1824 he said, 'The sun and the moon are scarcely more different from each other than Cambridge is from what it was when I was first Minister of Trinity Church; and the same change has taken place through almost the whole land.'[31] In 1829 he reminisced to one of his conversation parties that thirty years earlier 'five hundred pounds could not have collected such a party' as surrounded him there. He said 'it was a university crime to speak to me'.[32] In the last third of his life, attendance at his Sunday evening services averaged about two hundred and fifty undergraduates.[33] In other words, a large percentage of the total student population were sitting directly under his teaching.[34] His influence on undergraduates in general, and upon ordination candidates in particular, was phenomenal.[35] Lord Macaulay was at Cambridge towards the end of Simeon's life and he wrote to his sister, 'If you knew what his authority and influence were, and how they extended from Cambridge to the most remote corners of England, you would allow that his real sway in the Church was far greater than that of any Primate.'[36] It would be difficult to underestimate the significance of Simeon's ministry to university students over such a prolonged period and it is surprising that in Wolffe's recent history of Evangelicalism in this period Simeon

---

[29] Hopkins, *Charles Simeon of Cambridge*, p 86.
[30] Cited in Hopkins, *Charles Simeon of Cambridge*, p 68.
[31] Carus, *Memoirs of the Life*, p 415.
[32] Hopkins, *Charles Simeon of Cambridge*, p 84.
[33] Ford Brown, *Fathers of the Victorians*, p 295.
[34] Even if we take into account the fact that the number of students at the university had doubled from 1811 to 1827 this is still a considerable percentage, Pollock, *A Cambridge Movement*, p 9.
[35] Hylson-Smith, *Evangelicals in the Church of England*, p 74.
[36] George M. Trevelyan, *Life and Letters of Lord Macaulay* (London: Longmans Green, 1881), p 50 fn.

does not feature more prominently.[37] On any historical assessment it must be concluded that Simeon's was a remarkable ministry. But was its impact only felt in Simeon's day and in the lives he personally ministered to or has he continued to exercise influence down to today?

5.2. What Sprang From Simeon's Ministry?

To suggest that Simeon was the founder of Evangelical university ministry is by no means novel. Many histories of student Christian unions begin with some account of Simeon's ministry and the development of student ministry over subsequent decades.[38] The story is told of how, in response to a sermon Simeon preached in 1827, a group of Cambridge students began a Sunday school to poor children in Jesus Lane. A generation later, in 1862, a group of students who were actively involved in the Jesus Lane Sunday School began the Daily Prayer Meeting (DPM), which by 1875 had ten percent of students supporting it. The DPM had an evangelistic meeting once a term, and it was from this group that the Cambridge Inter-Collegiate Christian Union (CICCU) was formed. The CICCU then became a model for other student Christian groups throughout Britain and the world. As Prime surmised, 'Little could Simeon or his congregation have anticipated how significant that one sermon would prove to be.'[39]

After a series of challenges to the authority of Scripture and the centrality of the atonement in the early years of the twentieth century, the CICCU disaffiliated from the more liberal inter-university Student Christian Movement (SCM).[40] At the end of the First World War, after an attempt at reconciliation demonstrated that the move away from

---

[37] There are only eight passing references to Simeon in Wolffe's account of the expansion of Evangelicalism and he does not deal specifically with Simeon's work at all. John Wolffe, *The Expansion of Evangelicalism: The Age of Wilberforce, More, Chalmers and Finney* (Nottingham: IVP, 2006).

[38] Pollock, *A Cambridge Movement*, p 1-12, Douglas Johnson, *Contending for the Faith: A History of the Evangelical Movement in Universities and Colleges* (Leicester: IVP, 1979), pp 32-37, *Christ and the Colleges: A History of the Inter-Varsity Fellowship of Evangelical Unions*, ed. Donald Coggan (London: IVF, 1934), p 12, Prime, *Charles Simeon*, p 239-40, Pete Lowman, *The Day of His Power: A History of the International Fellowship of Evangelical Students* (Leicester: IVP, 1983), p 19, Meredith Lake, *Proclaiming Jesus Christ as Lord: A History of the Sydney University Evangelical Union* (EU Graduates Fund, 2005), p 2.

[39] Prime, *Charles Simeon*, p 240.

[40] Pollock, *A Cambridge Movement*, pp 159-189, 193-218.

Evangelical fundamentals had become entrenched in the SCM, the Inter-Varsity Fellowship (IVF) was established as an alternative national body for Evangelical students. Geraint Fielder highlighted that this did not necessarily mean things went from strength to strength for the new movement. Indeed, he said, 'The centenary of Charles Simeon's death in 1936 could hardly have marked a lower tide in the ebb and flow of fidelity to the Scriptures.'[41] And yet, although embattled on numerous fronts, the IVF and the CICCU in particular still looked back to Simeon for inspiration. John Stott, an undergraduate at Cambridge in the early 1940s remembered being introduced to the story of Simeon through his involvement in the CICCU.[42] After the Second World War, in 1947, the IVF affiliated with other Evangelical student bodies under the banner of the International Fellowship of Evangelical Students (IFES). This body now encompasses Christian Unions in more than 130 countries.

In terms of the IVF's reach into Australia, it was the charismatic doctor turned preacher, Howard Guinness, who came to the country in 1930 to help establish Evangelical Unions among students of Sydney and Melbourne Universities.[43] Evangelical Unions soon began at several other Australian universities and by 1936 they joined together in the Australian Inter-Varsity Fellowship.[44] Meredith Lake has shown how the Sydney University Evangelical Union (SUEU) identified with Simeon and the Cambridge tradition from its earliest days. She claims that the fledgling Union celebrated the Cambridge tradition as an encouragement to evangelize and as a mechanism of coping with atheism and liberalism.[45] Furthermore, she demonstrates that subsequent SUEU students also valued the Simeon tradition, as, for example, members handbooks throughout the 1960s recounted his story as the beginning of modern student Christian work and thus also

---

[41] Geraint Fielder, *Lord of the Years: Sixty Years of Student Witness* (Leicester: IVP, 1988), p 67.

[42] Timothy Dudley-Smith, *John Stott: The Making of a Leader* (Leicester: IVP, 1999), p 188, Steer, *Church on Fire*, p 168.

[43] Howard Guinness, 'Australia', in *Christ and the Colleges: A History of the Inter-Vasity Fellowship of Evangelical Unions* (London: IVF, 1934), pp 169-88. John Prince and Moyra Prince, *Out of the Tower* (Sydney: ANZEA Publishers, 1987), pp 8-15, Lake, *Proclaiming*, pp 15-16, Fielder, *Lord of the Years*, pp 42-44. Lowman, *The Day of His Power*, pp 54-68, For more detail about Guiness at Melbourne University see *Decisive Years: Experiences of Christian University Students*, ed. David Angus (Melbourne, 2005), pp 2-6.

[44] Lake, *Proclaiming*, p 16.

[45] Lake, *Proclaiming*, p 28.

of the SUEU.[46] Interestingly, Lake also highlights that in the periods of the SUEU's history when engagement with social issues gained priority over faithfulness to Scripture and evangelism, there was a corresponding distancing from Simeon and the Cambridge tradition.[47] Nevertheless, it is fairly easy to trace a legacy of ministry amongst students in Australia back to Simeon's ministry in Cambridge, but has he been influential in a more direct way on the shape of contemporary university ministry?

5.3. *Phillip Jensen's Ministry at UNSW*[48]

I would like to answer this question by examining the remarkable twenty-eight year ministry at The University of New South Wales (UNSW) led by Revd Phillip Jensen. By the time Jensen moved from his role as chaplain of UNSW and rector of St Matthias to become Dean of Sydney in 2003, thousands of students had sat under his teaching in Campus Bible Study (CBS) and St Matthias Church had grown from a few dozen people to sixteen congregations numbering over a thousand people.[49] Although the work of Simeon did not factor in Jensen's approach as he began his university ministry, there were numerous parallels between their experiences. Nevertheless, after the ministry of CBS had been established, Jensen 'discovered' Simeon's work and it influenced him in a couple of significant ways.

A simple comparison of the early stages of Simeon's ministry at Cambridge and Jensen's ministry at UNSW reveals some uncanny similarities. Both men were placed in their ministry at the direction of their bishop. In both cases this was against the will of the existing congregation. In both cases the congregations mounted opposition to the ministry. In both cases the wider university was also hostile to an Evangelical witness. Both men sought to make expository preaching the

---

46 Lake, *Proclaiming,* p 28.
47 She gives the example of the SUEU Members Handbook, Feb 1971, Lake, *Proclaiming.* pp 28,37.
48 Unless otherwise footnoted, all quotes in this section derive from an interview with Phillip Jensen on 6 May 2015. Peter Bolt's forthcoming biography of P D Jensen will provide a much fuller account of the particular events surrounding Jensen's arrival and early ministry at UNSW.
49 'St Matthias, Draft Parish Profile', 31 January 2003, Hodkinson: 20.123. states that 'By mid-2002, some fifteen different congregations had been planted across the Eastern Suburbs, Inner West, and Inner South, with over 1400 members and regulars attending.' The Campus Bible Study was serving 600 students per week.

foundation of their ministry. Both men's deep desire was to see students converted. Both men sought to train students in theology by smaller groups where questions were answered. (It is remarkable how similar the format of Jensen's early Ministry Training Strategy (MTS) training sessions resembled Simeon's conversation parties.) Both men were focused on sending convicted Evangelicals into full time ministry and training up preachers of the gospel. Even the terms of derision used against students that were part of their ministry were similar... 'Simeonite' and 'Jensenite'. And yet, in none of these parallels had Jensen consciously used Simeon as a model. Reflecting on this, Jensen believes that it was their shared Evangelical theology that led them to similar practices and experiences. The argument in this paper, however, is not that Simeon's ministry was *similar* to Australian university ministry, but rather, that he has been an enduring influence.

In one sense, I had hoped that when I went to interview Philip Jensen he would have said that he read about Simeon as a Moore College student and through this reading he felt God calling him to a university ministry based on evangelism and expository preaching which radically changed the direction of his life. Well, unfortunately for this chapter that was not the case! Jensen's ministry at UNSW took shape quite independently of Simeon. Yet, after Jensen's work was underway, he bought a copy of Hopkins' biography of Simeon. His reflection on reading it was,

> It blew me away... When I read what he did, it was what I was doing. He met on Friday nights, he expounded passages of Scripture, he didn't mind what others were saying, he wrote up outlines of sermons... He was recruiting young men to go the mission field... his idea of filling all the pulpits he could with Evangelical preachers, having trained them in teaching the Bible was what I was doing...

This was a wonderful realisation for Jensen. He says, 'It was part gratitude, part joy, part excitement to find that all my 'creativity' had a precedent two hundred years earlier'. Jensen described reading the book as like finding a friend who understood him. But there was one important aspect of Simeon that Jensen apprehended in reading Hopkins' biography which significantly influenced the shape of his university ministry.

When Jensen began at UNSW in 1975, chaplains to the university were given four year contracts. Jensen himself had agreed to these terms but at the end of 1977 Jensen went to see the Archbishop of Sydney to suggest that he should finish his contract a year early. His thinking behind this was that Billy Graham was coming in 1979 and it was important for the next chaplain to be well established before the Crusade. The Archbishop encouraged Jensen to stay on, even beyond the end of his contract, in order to maximise the evangelistic opportunity of Graham's visit. At this point it is worth pondering for a moment how ministry at UNSW might have been different if Jensen had finished up after just three years?

It must have been about this time that Jensen read the Hopkins' 1977 biography of Simeon. It revolutionised his thinking on the longevity of ministry. In his words,

> From the day I read that book, I just kept on seeing how Simeon did what he did, and how big the impact was because of his continuity in the doing of it. How stupid it was to have chaplains for four years!... [I saw that] the longer I could hang on into this situation, the more people I could keep impacting by doing what Simeon did, that is, the same thing all the time.

For the work at UNSW for the next several decades under Jensen's leadership, this was a hugely significant realisation. In his words, '[Simeon] did encourage me to stay longer and to be single minded in the task.' The longevity of Jensen's university ministry did not only shape the way things were done at UNSW, but the Australian Fellowship of Evangelical Students (AFES) movement as a whole. Many university campuses across Australia continue to have an Evangelical ministry that is influenced by Jensen's work at UNSW.

A second influence Simeon had on Jensen was in helping him to see the massive advantage of ministry to residential students. In turn, Jensen began to prioritise the residential ministry because of the great influence he could have there. He said, 'Knowing that [Simeon's] impact came from being in a residential university helped me see the impact that could be had with residential students.' Indeed, the total number of residential students at UNSW in Jensen's time was similar to the total number of students at Cambridge in Simeon's time. Residence provided numerous teaching opportunities that commuting students missed. It was seeing the way Simeon used this experience that clarified Jensen's priority on these students.

After Jensen's 'discovery' of Simeon, the Cambridge precedent entered into the CBS narrative. Jensen read all that he could about Simeon. Particularly with the MTS trainees and staff workers, Jensen would point to Simeon as an example to follow. He emphasised Simeon's faithfulness to Scriptural exposition. He pointed to Simeon's patient endurance in the face of opposition. And all importantly, Jensen highlighted the profound impact of a long term strategic ministry.[50] Although working on the other side of the world, in a vastly different context, Simeon's university ministry was continuing to have an influence.

5.4.   *Conclusion*

Charles Simeon was an Evangelical stalwart of profound and lasting significance. He saw his ministry in Cambridge as of particularly strategic importance. He believed that through faithful and systematic exposition of the Bible the Lord would bring people into his kingdom and grow them in faith. He was particularly interested in training future leaders of the church in preaching and theology. He has rightly been seen as the founder of Evangelical ministry amongst university students – even university students on the other side of the world. But we have seen that his influence is far greater than merely a founder. The example of Phillip Jensen demonstrates the personal impact that Simeon's ministry has had. From Simeon, Jensen saw the gospel impact of long-term university ministry and residential student ministry. These insights shaped Jensen's own ministry at UNSW, a ministry that has itself become programmatic for other university ministries around Australia. Charles Simeon's ministry in Cambridge was 200 years and 17,000 km away from Phillip Jensen's ministry at UNSW, but their shared theology and practice, their common goal of training the next generation of gospel workers and the profound impact their ministries were to have lead us to conclude the distance from King's College to Kingsford is not so far at all.

---

[50]   These three lessons were recollected by Tony Payne, one of Jensen's MTS trainees in the mid-1980s. Conversation with Payne 20 February 2015.

6. Moderate Biblicism: How Charles Simeon's Theology Shaped His Relationship to the Church of England, Non-Conformists, and the Dissenter Movements – *James Snare*

Charles Simeon's ministry (1783-1836) covered a period of time when the Church of England faced sectarianism on various fronts. Calvinism was the dominant perspective but Arminianism was a growing influence. Dissatisfaction with the Established Church led many Evangelicals to break regular church order to the degree that they became known as Non-Conformists. Others left the Church of England altogether and formed various Dissenter movements, starting and joining churches outside of the Established Church. In this context, Simeon developed his theological outlook, including his Biblicism, a moderate theological approach and a desire for gospel unity. By looking at several examples of Simeon's relationship with the Church of England, Dissenters and Non-conformists, it becomes clear how Simeon's theological thinking shaped these associations. This provides an insight into how, at least in part, he helped preserve and grow the Evangelical movement in England and beyond.

6.1. *Simeon's Approach to Theological Differences*

The best way to understand Simeon's theological outlook is to begin with his Biblicism. In general, Simeon preferred Christians not to commit to a particular systematic theology but rather to commit to being biblical Christians. He said,

> Calvinism is a system. God has not revealed His truth in a system; the Bible has no system as such. Lay aside system and fly to the Bible; receive its words with simple submission, and without an eye to any system. Be Bible Christians and not system Christians.[1]

However Simeon did not believe that the Scriptures are without a system. He wrote that he had 'no doubt that there is a system in the Holy Scriptures; (for truth cannot be inconsistent with itself),' but he was 'persuaded that neither Calvinists nor Arminians are in exclusive possession of that system'.[2] It was significant for Simeon that God has

---

[1]   Abner Brown, *Recollections*, p 269.

[2]   Simeon, *Horae Homileticae* I, p 5.

not revealed himself by a system. Therefore the development of a comprehensive theological system was not to be people's prime theological concern. Pursuing it as a prime concern only invited trouble. He said,

> It is impossible to reduce the Holy Scriptures either to the one or to the other of them [Calvinism and Arminianism]: for, on both hypotheses, there are difficulties which can never be surmounted, and contrarieties which man can never reconcile. It is by attempting to be wise above what is written, that we involve ourselves in all these difficulties.[3]

Simeon therefore saw no obligation on preachers systematically to reconcile every part of the Scriptures to another.[4]

Simeon did think, however, that reconciliation of a sort is found in the pastoral application of the Scriptures. He believed that the correct scriptural response to apparently contradicting doctrine is

> not in an exclusive adoption of either, nor yet in a confused mixture of both, but in the proper and seasonable application of them both; or, to use the language of Paul, 'in rightly dividing the word of truth.'[5]

So in Scripture Simeon believed there is 'perfect agreement between these different points; and that they are equally salutary or equally pernicious, according as they are properly or improperly implied.'[6] Thus, for Simeon, apparently opposite tenets of Scripture can be 'profitably insisted upon'.[7]

In examining Simeon's theology, recent commentators have often identified the theme of 'balance'. Alan Munden comments that in contrast to the more sectarian systematic thinkers of his day, Simeon preferred a 'teaching that was more balanced'.[8] Derek Prime's recent biography calls his chapter on Simeon's theology 'Simeon and the Principle of Balance'.[9] Finally, Lee Gatiss in the 2014 St Antholin

---

3   Charles Simeon, *Horae Homileticae or Discourses (in the Form of Skeletons) upon the Whole Scriptures* (London: Richard Watts, 1819), XVIII. Discourse 2228.
4   Simeon, *Horae Homileticae* I, p xv.
5   Simeon, *Horae Homileticae* I, p xv.
6   Simeon, *Horae Homileticae* I, p xviii.
7   Simeon, *Horae Homileticae* I, p xvi.
8   Alan Munden, 'Charles Simeon, 1759-1836', in *The Heart of Faith: Following Christ in the Church of England*, ed. Andrew Atherstone (Cambridge: Lutterworth, 2008), p 83.
9   Prime, *Charles Simeon*, p 180.

Lectures thought that what Simeon was attempting to do in his theology was pastorally to blend Calvinism and Arminianism to achieve a 'supposedly better, more biblical, balance'.[10] It must be asked though if 'balance' is the best type of language to describe Simeon's theological thinking. The language of balance is not typical of the language Simeon uses to outline his theological method. In fact it is entirely absent from the clearest exposition of his own theological position; the preface to his *Horae Homileticae*.[11] It is also not the language he uses to describe himself in his correspondence to friends. Nor is it the language that is used to describe his position by those who knew him best (with one notable exception which is examined below). Admittedly, he speaks of the 'equality' of all Scripture in both authority and importance. However this is a different idea from creating a more balanced systematic theology or having a need constantly to balance out one part of Scripture with another. These approaches would be the antithesis of the position Simeon was attempting to outline.[12]

The better language to describe Simeon's approach to theology is that of 'moderation'. This is the language that Simeon and his friends themselves used to describe his approach. In a letter to Bishop Yorke who was concerned about Simeon's methods he wrote,

> In all matters that form a ground of difference between persons of real piety, I think I have endeavoured to exercise caution and *moderation*, but in truths of fundamental importance, I have thought it my duty to speak with firmness and energy.[13]

It has been rightly noted that Simeon did not usually identify himself with the systems of Calvinism or Arminianism, but when he did he used the language of moderation as a qualifier. In a letter to his friend and biographer William Carus he wrote he was a 'moderate Calvinist'.[14] Daniel Wilson, Bishop of Calcutta, was a friend and student of Simeon,

---

10 Lee Gatiss, *Strangely Warmed: Whitfield, Toplady, Simeon and Wesley's Arminian Campaigns* (London: Latimer, 2014), p 21.

11 'For if only here and there a sentence were culled from the sermons, which are studiously compressed into the smallest space, my views might possibly be mistaken; but in the preface they are brought to a point, in such a manner, that they cannot possibly be misunderstood.' Simeon, 'Letter to Bishop Yorke', 10 February 1809. Cited in Carus, *Memoirs of the Life*, p 197.

12 Simeon, *Horae Homileticae* I, pp. xiv–xviii.

13 Simeon, 'Letter to Bishop Yorke'. Cited in Carus, *Memoirs of the Life*, p 198.

14 Simeon, 'Letter to Revd W Carus Wilson', 11 October 1815. Cited in Carus, *Memoirs of the Life*, p 294. Simeon was not the only Evangelical to take the title of 'Moderate Calvinism' cf. Bebbington, *Evangelicalism in Modern Britain*, pp 63-65.

who when describing Simeon's thought leaned heavily on the language of moderation. He said,

> [Simeon's] Moderation on contested and doubtful points of Theology contributed to his ultimate success – not moderation in the sense of tameness as to the great vital truths of the Gospel – not moderation as implying conformity to the world's judgment of Christian doctrine – but the true scriptural moderation arising from a sense of man's profound ignorance, and of the danger of attempting to proceed one step beyond the fair and obvious import of Divine Revelation. In this sense he was a moderate.[15]

For Simeon then, moderation in theology was an essential value for Christians to hold onto when addressing issues of doctrine that were not core gospel truths. Simeon's goal was not to achieve a balance between seemingly contradictory doctrines of Scripture. Nor was it to develop a more balanced blend of Calvinism and Arminianism. Rather, he wanted all systematic thinking to be done with a moderate approach. What this meant was ensuring that a system did not develop to the point where the plain, literal sense of some passages of Scripture were ignored or had to be overcome in order to fit within a man-made doctrinal scheme. As Wilson stated, this was based on his anthropology which saw distinct restrictions on humanity's ability to reconcile what God himself has not clearly explained to us. He held therefore that people had a limited capacity to discern harmony and agreement between apparently conflicting Scriptures.[16]

Importantly, this moderate approach did not extend to all areas of doctrine and certainly not to fundamental truths of the gospel. On these there was no room for anything but 'energy and firmness'. The primacy of foundational gospel truths was central to Simeon's theological convictions and significant for his ecclesiology. Munden is right to say that while Simeon admitted that those who call themselves Christians held a variety of views about religion, 'he made it clear that *real* Christians agreed about the fundamentals.'[17] For Simeon, the true believer 'feels himself to be a sinner before God; dependent altogether on the blood of Christ to purge him from his guilt, and on the Spirit of Christ to renew and sanctify his soul. The necessity of universal

---

15 Carus, *Memoirs of the Life*, p 593
16 Simeon, *Horae Homileticae* I, p xv.
17 Munden, 'Charles Simeon, 1759-1836', p 180.

holiness, too, is equally acknowledged by all.'[18] Samuel Thodey, one of the dissenting ministers in Cambridge, wrote in Simeon's obituary that

> He laid great stress in his preaching upon the depravity of human nature, the divinity and atonement of Christ, the justification of a sinner exclusively through the merits and righteousness of the Redeemer, the necessity of agency of the Holy Spirit to restore the divine image, and final perseverance.[19]

Wilson described Simeon's views by saying Simeon believed

> a clergyman must hold the same doctrines of the Fall and the Recovery of man – of the Atonement of Christ, and the operations of the Spirit – of justification by faith, and regeneration and progressive sanctification by grace – of holy love to God and man, and of all good works as the fruit of faith, and following after justification.[20]

To guard the centrality of these core gospel truths he was keen to ensure that as Christians thought about doctrine they did not mistake the foreground for the background. He was 'anxious that his friends should realise 'the great scope' of the divine revelation, and not be side-tracked from it.'[21] Accordingly he wrote to Ellen Elliot, granddaughter of Henry Venn, who had become interested in premillennialism: 'I have no objection to your believing the personal reign of Christ and his saints: I object to the prominence given to it, and to its thrusting into the background all the wonders of redeeming love.'[22] Indeed, the words Simeon chose for himself to appear on his own epitaph were the apostle Paul's, 'I determined not to know anything among you save Jesus Christ, and him crucified.'[23] So it is right to conclude that Simeon's moderate approach to theology resulted in a foreground/background framework to his thinking. In the foreground were the essential truths of Christ crucified, the depravity of man, salvation through Christ alone, the atonement, justification, sanctification by the Holy Spirit and the importance of persevering to the end. All other issues for him became background issues. Christians can 'let smaller differences of sentiment

---

18 Charles Simeon, *Horae Homileticae or Discourses (in the Form of Skeletons) upon the Whole Scriptures* (London: Richard Watts, 1819), XVII, p 339.
19 Quoted in Hopkins, *Charles Simeon of Cambridge*, p 180.
20 Carus, *Memoirs of the Life*, p 588.
21 Quoted in Hopkins, *Charles Simeon of Cambridge*, p 187.
22 Quoted in Hopkins, *Charles Simeon of Cambridge*, p 187.
23 Hopkins, *Charles Simeon of Cambridge*, p 180.

be overlooked, and all unite in vindicating the great doctrines of Salvation by Grace through Faith in Christ.'[24]

This issue of gospel unity was incredibly important to Simeon. The reason that Simeon gave for wanting to outline his theology clearly in his preface to *Horae Homileticae* was, 'to counteract that spirit of animosity, which has of late so greatly prevailed against those who adhere to the principles of the Established Church.'[25] His hope was that his work would not 'strengthen a party in the church, but...promote the good of the whole.'[26] Simeon was convinced that 'there is not anything more injurious to the Church of God than a party-spirit.'[27] He wanted 'to prevent bitterness in controversy, and the magnifying of non-essentials; to smooth down asperities of conflicting opinion, and resist the pride of party views.'[28] In particular Simeon believed that ministers should 'guard against adopting the shibboleth of a party, or the dogmas of any particular sect.'[29] For Simeon, 'Schism is a great evil. It is the separating of a part of the body of Christ; not a division among more professing Christians, but amongst real Christians.'[30]

Simeon was especially aware of the dangers involved in arguments between those who agreed on most things. He understood that these types of disagreement could be much more intense than those who disagreed on everything. He was therefore keen to promote a view that emphasized what could be agreed upon. These words were part of a letter that brought to a close a public argument Simeon had with a Dr. Pearson of Cambridge in the *Christian Advocate*,

> Persons who have the same general design, but differ in some particular modes of carrying it into execution, often stand more aloof from each other, than they do from persons of whose principles and conduct they entirely disapprove. Hence prejudice arises, and a tendency to mutual crimination: whereas if they occasionally conversed for half an hour with each other, they would soon rectify their mutual misapprehensions, and concur in aiding,

---

24 Simeon, *Horae Homileticae* I, p xxii.
25 Simeon, *Horae Homileticae* I, p xxi.
26 Simeon, *Horae Homileticae* I, p xxii.
27 Charles Simeon, *Horae Homileticae*, XVI, p 109.
28 Abner Brown, *Recollections*, pp 61-62.
29 Simeon, *Horae Homileticae* XVI, p 56.
30 Abner Brown, *Recollections*, p 224.

rather than undermining, the efforts of each other for public good.[31]

Despite his desire for unity, it is important to note that Simeon was by no means a subscriber to the idea of unity at all costs. When writing to a friend who was working under a hostile Bishop, Simeon advised the Revd Richardson, 'Circumstanced as you are, I feel no hesitation in saying, that you should avoid everything that can give offence, except faithful preaching of 'Christ Crucified.'[32] Simeon was keen to avoid unnecessary fights but on the topic of the gospel he believed one must stand firm in his conviction even if it caused offense. Similarly, when listening to those who risked departing from gospel orthodoxy, Simeon was a keen listener and careful about whom he expressed agreement with. In an anecdote told by Joseph Romilly, Simeon's concern for gospel orthodoxy is clear. Listening to the controversial Dissenter Edward Irving, Simeon heard him with 'a fixed resolve to say Amen to nothing that he had not well sifted and deliberately approved'. In Simeon's look was as much 'sober reproof, exhortation and caution as a look could convey.'[33]

Given his commitment to gospel unity it is unsurprising that Simeon was no great sympathizer with the central tenets and philosophy of the Non-Conformist and Dissenter movements, especially when it came to their reasoning to break away from the Church of England. He regarded Dissent and schism as great evils.[34] Simeon saw weaknesses in Protestant Nonconformity, including its lack of liturgy, its bias to disunion, and its 'censorious, judicial spirit' evinced in the tyranny of the people over their pastors.[35] However in his relationships and partnerships with people Simeon was still primarily concerned to determine where a person's commitment lay in regards to the foundational doctrines of the gospel. This was much more important than their commitment to a particular system or indeed, even to the Church of England as an institution. Archbishop Coggan declared, 'If a

---

[31] Simeon, 'Letter to Dr Pearson', 1810. Cited in Carus, *Memoirs of the Life*, p 208.

[32] Simeon, 'Letter to Revd Mr. Richardson', 7 March 1814. Cited in Carus, *Memoirs of the Life*, p 272.

[33] Quoted in Hopkins, *Charles Simeon of Cambridge*, p 233.

[34] Abner Brown, *Recollections*, p 224.

[35] Charles Smyth, *Simeon and Church Order: A Study in the Evangelical Revival in Cambridge in the Eighteenth Century* (London: Cambridge, 1940), p 290; Abner Brown, *Recollections*, pp 223-224.

man loved Christ, Simeon grasped hands with him.'[36] Simeon believed the principles of the Established church to be right and the dissenters mistaken but as long as they loved Jesus, Simeon could embrace them. Abner Brown wrote, 'He did not merely deem the Church preferable to Nonconformity, but honestly believed the Church right, and the principles of Dissent wrong; while yet his catholic spirit could embrace all who sincerely loved and served the Lord Jesus Christ.'[37]

First and foremost though, Simeon wanted to keep people in the Church of England. Simeon was proud of the fact that after thirty years of ministry at Holy Trinity, he had only lost three people of maturity to the Dissenters.[38] At times he would even borrow from the methods of the Dissenters if he thought it would help him to ensure that people remained within the Established Church. In regards to his 'illegal conventicles' he defended the practice with reference to the methods of the Dissenters and the Methodists in particular. He argued,

> The Dissenters in general, and the Methodists in particular, have such meetings; and they are found to be of the highest utility for the cultivation of mutual love, and for the keeping of their respective members in one compact body ... experience proves that wherever there is an efficient ministry in the Church without somewhat of a similar superintendence, the clergyman beats the bush and the Dissenters catch the game: whereas where such superintendence is maintained the people are united as an army with banners.[39]

Simeon's gospel unity was clearly centred then on the Church of England.

To summarise his theological position, it is best to say that Simeon's Biblicism led to his rejection of what he saw to be over-developed theological systems. Instead he encouraged Christians to turn to the Bible and not man-made doctrinal schemes. Simeon's theology was not a search for balance but rather a moderate approach to theology that was driven by his anthropology. He did not believe man could fully

---

36 Donald Coggan, *These Were His Gifts* (Exeter: University of Exeter, 1974), p 16; Quoted in, Andrew Atherstone, 'Evangelical Mission and Anglican Church Order: Charles Simeon Reconsidered', in *Preachers, Pastors, and Ambassadors: Puritan Wisdom for Today's Church: St. Antholin Lectures 2001-2010*, ed. by Lee Gatiss (London: Latimer Trust, 2011), p 372.
37 Abner Brown, *Recollections*, p 12.
38 Carus, *Memoirs of the Life*, p 109.
39 Carus, *Memoirs of the Life*, p 109.

understand whatever system was at work within the Scriptures. Instead Christians should focus on the primary and essential truths of the great doctrines of salvation by grace through faith. He had a real desire for gospel unity and wanted to address the sectarian spirit he saw within the Church of England. To do so he taught Christians to take the focus off background theological issues of secondary importance and to refocus on the great scope of scripture, the gospel. Importantly this desire for gospel unity was grounded in his desire for people to be a part of the Church of England. This desire fits well with his Biblicism which will become apparent through a consideration of his relationship the Church of England.

6.2.   Simeon's Moderate Approach in Relationship to Others

6.2.1.   The Church of England

Armed with a clear understanding of Simeon's broad theological approach, it is worth taking some time to examine in turn how Simeon's theology played out in his relationship to the Church of England, the Dissenters and the Non-Conformists. First, the Church of England; Simeon's love for the Established Church, despite its problems, is well known. It has been said that Simeon 'loved the Church of England. He loved its liturgy. And he was content to live and die a son of the Church of England, even though within that church he suffered so much and saw so much that was weak and unworthy in its priests and people.'[40] Indeed Simeon's love for the Established Church was so great that at times he was criticized for being 'more of a Church-man than a gospel man' and that 'His trumpet gives an uncertain sound' when it came to the gospel.[41] Even in modern times Simeon has been claimed as a hero of church law over any form of irregularity in regards to church order.[42] The common picture painted in many Simeon biographies is that he is 'the archetypal obedient Anglican churchman.'[43]

---

40   Coggan, *These Were His Gifts*, p. 16; Quoted in, Atherstone, p 372.
41   Abner Brown, *Recollections*, p 11.
42   Graham Kings, 'Judicious or Precipitate? Evangelicals and Order in the Church of England', *Fulcrum Newsletter*, December 2005; Quoted in, Atherstone, 'Evangelical Mission and Anglican Church Order', p 370.
43   Atherstone, 'Evangelical Mission and Anglican Church Order', p 370.

However, Andrew Atherstone has argued convincingly that despite his deep love for the Church of England, Simeon's first priority was the essential truths of the gospel. Simeon's participation in activities that pushed the boundaries of church laws (if not outright breaking them) is evidence of this. His irregular preaching, his organization of illegal conventicles, his administration of autonomous Bible and mission societies and his quasi-episcopal ministry all demonstrate how, when presented with a choice between the secondary interests of church order and the primary interests of the gospel, he unfailingly made the gospel his priority.[44] Even Simeon's supposed retreats when faced with the censures of Church Order were done in order to preserve gospel ministry.[45]

Crucially, the reason that Simeon was so committed to the Church of England was because in its confessions he saw what he believed to be the best expression of the gospel truths and biblical foundations that he held to so dearly. Speaking of his own views he wrote,

> If in anything he grounded his sentiments upon human authority, it would not be on the dogmas of Calvin or Arminius, but on the Articles and Homilies of the Church of England. He has the happiness to say, that he does *ex animo*, from his inmost soul, believe the doctrines to which he has subscribed: but the reason of his believing them is not, that they are made the creed of the Established Church, but, that he finds them manifestly contained in the Sacred Oracles.[46]

So Simeon was a Church-man but only because in the Church of England's confessions and liturgy he saw the gospel and his decisions to obey, bend or break church order were decided in accordance with his commitment to gospel essentials.

6.2.2. Dissenting Christians

The second relationship to consider is Simeon's relationship with Joseph John Gurney. Gurney is a good example of Simeon's relationship with a gospel minded Dissenter. One of their encounters was helpfully recorded by Gurney and then copied into Carus' work on Simeon. The record takes on a slightly hagiographical tone but is an excellent source of insight into Simeon's thinking as it was recorded in

---

[44] Carus, *Memoirs of the Life*, pp 50, 40, 108; Atherstone. pp. 390-394.
[45] Carus, *Memoirs of the Life*, pp 240-241.
[46] Simeon, *Horae Homileticae* I, p xiv fn.

Gurney's journal the very same night that their conversation took place. Gurney was an Evangelical minister and an 'earnest and consistent member of the Society of Friends', otherwise known as the Dissenting group, the Quakers.[47] His Evangelical qualifications are historically supported by his commitment to the authority of Scripture which was demonstrated in his role in the Wilburite-Gurneyite Separation.[48]

Gurney wrote that in April 1831 the older Simeon was 'full of love towards all who love his Master and full of kindness for both the religious and the worldly.'[49] Their conversation was about 'the crude zeal of many' who had lost their balance in religion.[50] Gurney relates how Simeon spoke of his method of interpreting the Scriptures without seeking to impose a system upon them. Gurney comments that,

> If Christians universally adopted this principle of our friend's this 'new discovery' as I ventured to call it, how quickly would it terminate controversy, and put an end to polemical bitterness. We should all be brought into harmony of faith and doctrine. In the meantime, however, it is much to be lamented that Christians should judge one another.[51]

Elsewhere, Gurney is equally praiseworthy of Simeon's approach.[52] It is worth noting in light of Gurney's view of Simeon that Simeon himself could at times be quite critical of Quaker theology.[53] Despite their theological differences, however, Simeon knew that Gurney was committed to the Scriptures and the gospel and hence Gurney enjoyed

---

47 Joseph Brevan Braithwaite, *Memoirs of Joseph John Gurney with Selection from His Journal and Correspondence* (Norwich: Fletcher and Alexander, 1854), p iv.

48 This was a debate over the role of the Bible and hearing personally from the Holy Spirit that led to schism in the American Quaker movement. Stephen Ward Angell and Pink Dandelion, eds., *The Oxford Handbook of Quaker Studies* (1st ed.; Oxford Handbooks; Oxford: Oxford University, 2013), 71.

49 Carus, *Memoirs of the Life*, p 471.

50 This is the one reference to 'balance' made by Simeon's friends mentioned earlier. It is noteworthy that this is Gurney's word, not Simeon's, and that Simeon prefers to use the word 'impartial' in describing how he avoids subscribing to a particular doctrine over another. Balance, in the sense of weighing one doctrine against another, is still not the coordinating principle in Simeon's thinking.

51 Carus, *Memoirs of the Life*, p 472.

52 Simeon 'had no liking for new-fangled notions or strange flights in the things of God; but steadily pursued the old beaten path of Gospel-faith and Gospel practice.' Carus, *Memoirs of the Life*, p 480.

53 Simeon relates Quakers to two antinomian ministers and their divorce from the authority of the written Word. Carus, *Memoirs of the Life*, p 462.

Simeon's 'intimate affections'.[54] On at least one occasion Simeon stayed with Gurney when travelling to London for his work with the 'London Society for Converting the Jews'.[55] Furthermore the two walked in at least indirect gospel partnership through their respective work with the British and Foreign Bible Society.[56] So it seems that with Gurney, Simeon's commitment to the primacy of the gospel in a person's life meant he could walk in a solid relationship with him. Just as he would push the limits of the Established Church's order for the sake of the gospel, so too for the sake of the gospel, he would unite with those outside the Established church.

6.2.3. Non-Conformists

This is also seen in the way that his relationship changed over time with the notable Non-Conformist John Berridge. Historian Charles Smyth wrote of Berridge that, 'No Anglican incumbent of his day defied Church Order more violently than John Berridge, or with as much impunity.'[57] Berridge had some influence on Simeon early in his career and part of that was to encourage Simeon to participate in cross-Parish preaching which he did. If not for the influence of Henry Venn it is possible that Simeon might have followed Berridge into a much more committed form of irregularity in his ministry.[58] This makes sense as there was much in Berridge's ministry that Simeon approved of: his Evangelical fervour, his zeal, the pastoral sympathy and understanding, and his homely language. But there was much of which Simeon was critical too: his sermons had 'a very painful style and manner', his shouting and roaring at the ministry training practices of the Colleges, and above all his impatience with Church order.[59] While it is true Simeon turned away from following Berridge's path and would later look upon his early ministry with some regret, he notably maintained a close relationship with Berridge to the end.[60] He and Henry Venn used to go over and dine with John Berridge at Everton every Tuesday, and Simeon was eventually called to give the funeral sermon upon

54   Carus, *Memoirs of the Life*, p 471.

55   Carus, *Memoirs of the Life*, p 477.

56   Braithwaite, *Memoirs of Joseph John Gurney*, pp 446-449.

57   Smyth, *Simeon and Church Order*, p 250.

58   Smyth, *Simeon and Church Order*, pp 271-281.

59   Abner Brown, *Recollections*, pp 186-187, 193-194, 200-202; Smyth, *Simeon and Church Order*, p 270.

60   Carus, *Memoirs of the Life*, pp 199-200.

Berridge's death.[61] So, once again, this time with a notable Non-Conformist, Simeon enjoyed an intimate friendship with someone with whom he had clear differences. Importantly though, these differences were around secondary issues, specifically Berridge's approach to Church Order. What united them was their agreement over the essentials of the gospel, driven by Simeon's own foreground/background framework when thinking about Christian living and doctrine.

6.2.4. Simeon and Wesley

For a final insight into how his theology shaped his relationships, it is worth considering Simeon's most famous relationship with a Non-conformist. It consisted in only two recorded meetings but the names involved make it worthy of reflection. The first meeting between John Wesley and Simeon took place on December 20, 1784. Simeon specifically went to see Wesley to talk to him about the illicit conventicles that Simeon was holding outside his own parish. Wesley, being Wesley, unsurprisingly exhorted him to continue the gospel work that he was doing.[62] The second more famous exchange happened on Oct 30, 1787. The accuracy of the portrayal of this meeting can be questioned on the grounds that Simeon has structured it to show himself in a particularly positive light and furthermore, Simeon recorded the conversation approximately twenty years after the event itself. But Simeon says that the words recorded are very nearly the ones spoken at the time. So the fact that beyond its positive portrayal of Simeon and its odd stylistic structure there is no reason to doubt its basic accuracy means we should treat seriously this account as a reliable historical source.

In the conversation, Simeon asks the ageing Wesley about his basic depravity, his ability to turn to God without God acting first, his belief in salvation through Christ alone, remaining in salvation by works, the sustaining power of God to salvation, and his belief in God's preservation of him to the end. Wesley answers affirmatively to each of these inquiries and therefore satisfies any reasonable Calvinist's

---

[61] Henry Venn, *The Life and a Selection from the Letters*, p 519.

[62] Smyth, *Simeon and Church Order*, pp 286-287 The source for this meeting is a much later recollection of the event only published in 1814 but the basic shape of Simeon going to meet Wesley and Wesley encouraging the preaching of the gospel over strictly following church order fit well with both the character of the people and their times and on this level should be taken as accurate.

complaints about the great Arminian. Simeon then closes the exchange with these words in response to Wesley's answers,

> ... this is all my Calvinism; this is my election, my justification by faith, my final perseverance: it is in substance, all that I hold, and as I hold it: and therefore, if you please, instead of searching out grounds of contention between us, we will cordially unite in those things wherein we agree.[63]

What do these two encounters tell us? Clearly, the young Simeon was happy to seek counsel from Wesley on an issue of church order versus gospel priority despite Wesley's Arminianism, and status as a dissenter. Furthermore it should be noted that Simeon seeks grounds for unity rather than discord on those matters which Simeon holds to be the essentials of the doctrines of election, justification by faith and perseverance. Simeon's 'truce' with Wesley and the putting away of daggers is dependent on Wesley's satisfactory answers to each of Simeon's questions on what he saw as being gospel essentials. However, at this point, it is fair to ask whether Simeon's eagerness for a moderate approach to systematics, his Biblicism and his desire for gospel unity leads him somewhat astray from a typical reformed Evangelical perspective.

6.3. *An Evaluation of Simeon's Approach*

Simeon is at the very least reductionist in his approach to both Calvinism and Arminianism. In both his preface to *Horae Homileticae* and elsewhere, Simeon consistently reduces Calvinism to the doctrine of grace and the doctrine of perseverance and Arminianism to the doctrine of free will and the doctrine of non-perseverance. As Gatiss points out, the debate was much more complex than that. He writes that it is overly simplistic to act 'as if Calvinists...held to divine sovereignty but did not appeal for human decisions, or that they simply ignored parts of Scripture that did not at first blush seem to fit their preconceived system.'[64] In his *Institutes* Calvin certainly rejected the idea of 'free will' where man is thought to be 'master of both his own mind and will, able of his own power to turn himself toward either good or evil'.[65] However he did not deny the concept of human agency which

---

[63] Simeon, *Horae Homileticae* I, p xviii.

[64] Gatiss, *Strangely Warmed*, p 21.

[65] John Calvin, *Institutes of the Christian Religion: In Two Volumes*, ed. by John Thomas MacNeill, trans. by Ford Lewis Battles (London: Westminster John Knox, 1960), p II.ii.7.

seems to be what Simeon has in mind when he talks about free will. Simeon wrote, 'If the doctrines of Election and predestination be so stated as to destroy man's *free agency*, and make him merely passive in the work of salvation, they are not stated as they are in the Articles and Homilies of our Church, or as they are in the Holy Scriptures.'[66] This confusion of the doctrine of 'free will' and 'agency' in Simeon's works ignores Calvin's nuanced view of the faculty of the will and misrepresents the Calvinist perspective. It also seems to misunderstand the Arminian position of prevenient grace or 'universal enablement'. This seems to fly directly in the face of Simeon's own position that God must be recognized as both 'the *Author* and *Finisher* of our faith'.[67]

Simeon in his attempt to push for gospel unity has overlooked the 'real gospel minded concern at the heart of people's concerns about Wesley' which would call into question some of the essential truths that Simeon is so keen to champion.[68] While Gatiss mistakes Simeon's desire for reconciling biblical truths by rightly applying them pastorally for a desire to apply a pastoral blend of Calvinism and Arminianism, he is right to note that Simeon has possibly misread the significance of the Arminian doctrine of prevenient grace.[69] Simeon's desire to distinguish between foreground and background issues loses sight of the way that 'background issues' can be connected to and influence an understanding of foreground issues. The same could possibly be said about his approach to views such as Ellen Elliot's premillennialism.

At this point it is worth stepping back to see how the shaping of Simeon's relationships by his theological outlook fit the broader historical context. Historians have often concluded that Simeon was instrumental in keeping many Evangelicals within the Church of England and connected to the gospel truths that he saw expressed in its Articles and Homilies. Smyth wrote, 'I think we may confidently say that, without the steadying influence of Simeon at Cambridge, there would have been many more secessions that in fact occurred.'[70]

---

66 Simeon, *Horae Homileticae* I, p xviii.
67 Simeon, *Horae Homileticae* I, p xviii.
68 Gatiss, *Strangely Warmed*, p 23.
69 Gatiss incorrectly asserts that these words of Simeon are a reference to combining Calvinism and Arminianism. This is not the case. Rather, Simeon is referring to the two apparently contradicting points that are taken from John 5:40 where the responsibility to come to God is laid on men, and from John 6:44 where it said that no man can come to God unless the Father draws him near. Simeon, *Horae Homileticae* I, p xiv.
70 Smyth, *Simeon and Church Order*, p 255.

G M Trevelyan concurs and concludes that it was Simeon who put an end to the Evangelical drift into Non-Conformity.[71] Even within his own lifetime, and despite his personal desire to give all glory to God for the work that had been done, it was being recognised that Simeon deserved much credit for the increase of Evangelicalism in England.[72] Furthermore Simeon has been recognised as the person who, more than any other individual, took on the role of deciding where to draw the line on the issue of co-operation with Dissenters.[73] This role required a generous and thoughtful approach. What should be clear is that Simeon's success in being both generous and thoughtful can be traced back, at least in part, to his Biblicism, his moderate theological approach, and his desire for gospel unity. Each of these is demonstrated in his relationship with the Church of England, the Dissenters and the Non-Conformists. His reductionism when it came to Calvinism and Arminianism probably resulted in a misreading of the significance of issues like Wesley's Arminianism or the influence of a doctrine such as premillennialism. However his approach was mostly commendable and certainly fits with the picture of a man who was capable of keeping Evangelicals in the established church while simultaneously promoting gospel ministry outside of traditional church channels.

To conclude, Simeon's Biblicism, moderate theological approach, and focus on gospel unity defined his theological outlook. This theology shaped the way that he related to the Church of England, Dissenters and Non-Conformists. His focus on keeping the gospel in the foreground was the motivation for his commitment to the Church of England and his decisions to either obey, bend or brake Church order. This same approach allowed Simeon to disagree with the practices of the Non-Conformists but nevertheless maintain solid relationships with people like John Berridge and John Wesley. It also made it possible simultaneously to see great evil in dissension and schism and still to engage with Dissenters like J J Gurney. Simeon's approach in both his thinking and his relationships fits well with the qualities necessary to grow Evangelicalism within the Church of England while at the same time defining the relationship that the Church of England would have in gospel partnerships with those outside of the Established Church.

---

[71] George M. Trevelyan, *English Social History: A Survey of Six Centuries, Chaucer to Queen Victoria* (London: Longmans, 1942), p 510.

[72] Quoted in, Smyth, *Simeon and Church Order*, p 311.

[73] Smyth, *Simeon and Church Order*, p 290.

7. 'Loving in Deed and in Truth': The Practical Evangelicalism of Charles Simeon (1759-1836) – *David Furse-Roberts*

The title for this chapter is taken from the first Epistle of John who exhorted the children of God to not 'love in word or tongue but in deed and in truth'.[1] In the Evangelical world of eighteenth and nineteenth-century Britain, Charlies Simeon was one such disciple who took this command to heart, bearing much fruit in not only his own lifetime but in those of generations to follow. Born in Reading, Berkshire, in 1759 and converted to Evangelical Christianity under the influence of the Anglican clergyman, Henry Venn (1725-1797), Simeon devoted much of his life to consolidating Evangelicalism in the intellectual hub of Cambridge.[2] Much has been said about Simeon's manifold attributes as a teacher, a preacher, a pastor, an evangelist, a mission pioneer, a scholar, a visionary, and a clerical elder statesman. Indeed it would be accurate to say that Simeon was the consummate Evangelical who amply exhibited each of the four Evangelical characteristics famously identified by David Bebbington, namely those of conversionism, activism, biblicism and crucicentrism.[3]

7.1.   Simeon's Activist Evangelicalism

It is, however, the Evangelical trait of 'activism' that this paper focuses on with respect to Simeon and those who followed in his footsteps. According to Bebbington, the quality of activism was particularly pronounced in the role of an Evangelical minister and pastor, of whom Simeon was one for fifty-four years. Prior to the eighteenth-century Evangelical Revival led by Wesley and Whitefield, the role of a minister was primarily confined to taking services.[4] For Evangelicals such as Wesley, however, the post of minister was decidedly more *activist* with the devotion of many weekly hours to pastoral work amongst members of the congregation and the broader parish.[5] The primary impetus for this surge of activism amongst Evangelical clergy was the missionary

---

[1]   1 John 3:18
[2]   Gascoigne, *Cambridge in the Age of the Enlightenment*, pp 254-255.
[3]   Bebbington, *Evangelicalism in Modern Britain*, p 3.
[4]   Bebbington, *Evangelicalism in Modern Britain*, p 11.
[5]   Bebbington, *Evangelicalism in Modern Britain*, p 11.

impulse both to redeem the spiritual souls and to minister to the earthly bodies of people.

During his lengthy post at Holy Trinity Cambridge from 1783 to 1836, Simeon typified this activist impulse of Evangelicalism and it is a telling coincidence that Simeon was born in the same year as another celebrated Evangelical activist, William Wilberforce. As John Stott appreciated, these two exemplars of 'practical Christianity' knew each other and forged a warm lifelong friendship despite the Anglican layman and MP inhabiting a very different sphere from the clergyman of Cambridge.[6] Whilst Wilberforce's activism was primarily channelled through parliament and the public square, the theatres for Simeon's activism were always the parish church and mission society. Accordingly, it was in both his pastoral care of the parish poor and his contribution to domestic and overseas missionary enterprise that his activism was most pronounced.

Firstly, in his parish ministry, like Wesley before him, Simeon exhibited a palpable social conscience in his zeal to provide charitable relief to the poor in his midst. Whilst in Cambridge during the bread famine of 1788-89, Simeon contributed heavily to a scheme which enabled the destitute to obtain bread at half-price.[7] In a widely-circulated letter to leaders in each of the twenty-four villages dotted around Cambridge, Simeon wrote that for such schemes of poor relief to have good effect, they needed the aid of some gentleman in each village. Accordingly, he instructed these community leaders to table lists of people in their parishes that were most needy and then to hand this list to the minister on Sunday so that the distribution of aid by the parish church could be arranged.[8]   To ensure that this scheme was implemented, Simeon would ride into villages to see that the village bakers were performing their duty.[9]

Second, as was characteristic of his Evangelical contemporaries, Simeon was profoundly mission-orientated. With a vision to take the gospel abroad, he worked to establish voluntary societies committed to that end. Having being involved in discussions amongst the London

---

[6]   John Stott, 'Charles Simeon' (unpublished address, Taylor University, Upland, Indiana, U.S.A., 2004) <https://vimeo.com/17650814>.

[7]   Carus, *Memoirs of the Life*, p 80.

[8]   Simeon, 'Letter to the principal persons in each of the twenty-four villages near Cambridge', Kings College Cambridge, 17 January 1789. Cited in Carus, *Memoirs of the Life*, p 81.

[9]   Carus, *Memoirs of the Life*, p 80.

Eclectic Society on the most effective methods 'to promote the knowledge of the gospel among the heathen', the creation of the Church Missionary Society (CMS) represented one of his most tangible legacies. Founded in 1799, the new Society would be 'in direct connection with and under the sanction of the Church of England'.[10] Support and patronage of the Society was offered by Simeon's contemporaries, particularly Wilberforce, Henry Thornton and Thomas Scott.

As part and parcel of his missionary focus, Simeon entertained a special desire to promulgate the gospel in India, a concern he shared with his contemporary and Chair of the British East India Company, Charles Grant (1746-1823). In what he popularly referred to as 'facilitating the diffusion of Christian light in India',[11] Simeon made petitions and appeals to members of parliament to support his India endeavour, again gaining the support of Wilberforce, and his parliamentary protégé, Thomas F Buxton. Referring to India as his "diocese" or "province", Simeon managed, through his Cambridge connections, to recruit dozens of young clergy to serve overseas, as chaplains to the East India Company and as CMS missionaries.[12]

Embedded in Simeon's missionary matrix was also the project of proclaiming the gospel amongst the Jews, both at home and abroad. Simeon was said to have remarked that the conversion of the Jews was 'the most important object in the world'.[13] Certainly, an abiding commitment to this cause was reflected in his many sermons, journal entries and correspondence on the conversion and restoration of the Jewish people. Simeon would frequently write of his encouragement and delight from news that the New Testament had been distributed to Jews in Russia and Poland:

> The state of the Jews in Russia and Poland is very encouraging. Very many are anxious to have the New Testament in Hebrew; and if the Jews (two million of whom are in the Russian empire) can be furnished with that, there is reason to hope that many will find it the power of God to the salvation of their souls.[14]

---

[10]   Carus, *Memoirs of the Life*, p 166.
[11]   Simeon, 'Letter to the Revd T Thomason', 2 April 1813. Cited in Carus, *Memoirs of the Life*, p 362.
[12]   Munden, 'Charles Simeon, 1759-1836', p 87.
[13]   Munden, 'Charles Simeon, 1759-1836', p 87.
[14]   Simeon, 'Letter to the Revd T Thomason', Kings College Cambridge, 8 August 1817. Cited in Carus, *Memoirs of the Life*, pp 457-458.

To further this mission project at home, Simeon became a prominent leader of the London Society for Promoting Christianity amongst the Jews (LSPCJ) founded in 1809. As an enthusiastic leader within the Society, Simeon frequently attended committee meetings, spoke on numerous occasions at the annual meetings, preached deputation sermons and encouraged the formation of auxiliaries in parishes throughout the country.[15] Simeon's active contribution to both a pastorally sensitive and mission-focused Anglican Evangelicalism in his life-time was thus immeasurable.

7.2. *Simeon's Legacy for Australia*

With the British colonisation of Australian in 1788 coinciding with the burgeoning Evangelical movement in Britain, the Anglican Evangelical tradition epitomised by Charles Simeon was transplanted to Australian shores.[16] Recommended by the Eclectic Society to be appointed as chaplain to the First Fleet, the Reverend Richard Johnson (1753-1827) did much to sow the seed of faith in the new colony of Sydney Cove with his propagation of the Evangelical gospel famously preached by Simeon. Building on this foundation, the subsequent ministries of the Reverend Samuel Marsden (1764-1838) and Bishop Frederic Barker (1808-1882) gave the emerging Anglican Church of Sydney a decidedly Evangelical flavour. Steeped in this tradition of churchmanship, many of Sydney's clergy came to emulate Simeon's activist style of Evangelicalism in their ministries and we will now turn to explore three case studies spanning three generations. Like Simeon, each of these clergymen enjoyed lengthy vicarships of their respective parishes where they typified the 'activist' Evangelical characteristic described by Bebbington. There were indeed numerous other ministers in Sydney and beyond who mirrored Simeon's pastoral approach, but the following three cases are illustrative.

7.2.1. *Francis Bertie Boyce (1844-1931)*

The first was the clergyman and social reformer, Francis Bertie Boyce (1844-1931), who served various parishes in Bathurst, Orange and inner Sydney. Born in England only eight years after Simeon's death, Boyce drank from the same cistern of Anglican Evangelicalism and his parish

---

[15] Munden, 'Charles Simeon, 1759-1836', pp 87-88.
[16] Stuart Piggin, *Spirit of a Nation: The Story of Australia's Christian Heritage* (Sydney: Strand Publishing, 2004), p 5.

ministry bore recognisably similar fruit to that of Simeon. After emigrating from England to Australia in 1853, Boyce continued his education in Sydney before deciding to enter ministry in the Church of England. Trained at Moore Theological College in the 1860s, Boyce served in two rural parishes before his eventual appointment to St Paul's, Redfern, in 1884.[17] Like Simeon, he presided over a lengthy parish ministry, serving at St Paul's for forty-six years. Forever at the coalface of pastoral ministry, Boyce came into personal contact with many families living destitute lives in the slums that then populated many parts of the inner city. Boyce's practical Christianity impelled him to take action to bring both the gospel and the material necessity of adequate housing to the poor in his midst. Accordingly, in the 1890s, he called for the Sydney diocesan synod to set up a committee which would report to the church on the practical steps needed to address the spiritual and physical needs of impoverished city-dwellers.[18] Summing up his practical approach, Boyce wrote that it was 'the Master's work to preach the gospel in the slums; but it was equally his work to tear down the slums and to give His children clean, healthy and decent conditions under which to live.'[19] In addition to addressing Sydney's dire slum conditions, he successfully persuaded the Government of NSW to introduce the aged pension for the first time in 1901.[20] In the tradition of Simeon, Boyce believed that parish ministry was about tending to both the spiritual and physical needs of the people.

7.2.2. Robert Brodribb Stuart (RBS) Hammond (1870-1946)

Following the example of Archdeacon Boyce, another prominent Sydney minister who championed the practical Evangelicalism of Simeon was the towering figure of Robert Brodribb Stuart Hammond (1870-1946). Born in Victoria, Hammond was ordained in Melbourne in 1894 but moved to Sydney in 1899 to embark on a life of urban mission. Like Boyce, Hammond ministered in a number of inner-Sydney parishes where he was similarly moved by the plight of impoverished city-dwellers. Appointed to St Barnabas', Broadway, in 1918, Hammond transformed a dying parish into a powerhouse for evangelism and charitable enterprise.

---

[17] Kenneth J. Cable, 'Francis Bertie Boyce (1844-1931)', in *Australian Dictionary of Biography* (Melbourne: Melbourne University Press, 1979).

[18] Francis Bertie Boyce, *Fourscore Years and Seven: Memoirs of Archdeacon Boyce, for over Sixty Years a Clergyman of the Church of England in New South Wales* (Sydney: Angus and Robertson, 1934). p 87.

[19] Boyce, *Fourscore Years and Seven*, p 97.

[20] Boyce, *Fourscore Years and Seven*, pp 101-108.

Establishing an employment bureau, an emergency depot, a soup kitchen, eight hotels and family refuges, Hammond made his parish one of Sydney's primary centres for poor relief. Even before the Great Depression struck, St Barnabas' social service outlay exceeded £1,000, a figure unmatched by other Anglican parishes and agencies during the 1920s.[21] In the ensuing decades, Hammond's prodigious ministry of poor relief in his own parish was crowned by his project of establishing the Pioneer Homes Scheme, a charitable housing scheme for poor families that eventually evolved into the *HammondCare* charity. Reflecting on Hammond's legacy as recently as 2008, Archbishop Peter Jensen remarked that Hammond had 'fed the hungry, clothed the poor, uplifted the hopeless and fought against the drug trade while winning 4,400 men to Christ.'[22] According to Australian historian Meredith Lake, Hammond's ministry had integrated a typically Evangelical emphasis on personal sin, repentance, forgiveness and regeneration with an intense commitment to meeting material need'.[23] In this vein, he represented a worthy successor to both Charles Simeon and Archdeacon Boyce in his personification of practical Christianity.

7.2.3. *Bernard Judd (1918-1999)*

The final case study is that of Bernard Judd (1918-1999) who, appropriately, was both a protégé and successor of Hammond himself. Raised in Sydney's Chippendale, Judd worshipped at St Barnabas', Broadway, during the 1930s where he developed a fervent admiration for its rector, R B S Hammond.[24] Ordained an Anglican minister in 1942, Judd followed in the footsteps of Boyce and Hammond in his curacy of several inner-Sydney parishes before finally becoming rector of St Peter's, East Sydney, in 1947, where he served for thirty-nine years. Like his mentor, Judd divided his energies between serving the pastoral needs of his inner city parish and running the Hammond Pioneer Homes enterprise. Succeeding Hammond as the charity's director from the late 1940s, he similarly regarded social service and evangelism as mutually reinforcing activities of Christian ministry. Accordingly, he likened them to the two oars of a boat where each were necessary for propelling the

---

[21] Meredith Lake, 'Hammond, Robert Brodribb Stewart', in *Dictionary of Sydney*, 2012 <http://dictionaryofsydney.org/entry/hammond_robert_brodribb_stewart>.

[22] Peter Jensen, 'Presidential Address to Synod, 17 October 2008', *Year Book of the Diocese of Sydney 2009* (Diocesan Registry, Sydney) pp. 396-417, cited in Meredith Lake, *Faith in Action: Hammondcare* (Sydney: UNSW Press, 2013), p 26.

[23] Lake, *Faith in Action*, p 35.

[24] Lake, *Faith in Action*, pp 123-124.

church forward. He once commented that 'if a rower pulls one and neglects the other, he simply goes around in circles'.[25] In conjunction with his evangelism and mercy ministries, Judd emerged as a fearless champion for Christian moral truths in the public sphere together with the Dean of Sydney, Lance Shilton, in the 1970s and 80s.[26] While Judd's advocacy for temperance, sexual propriety and traditional family values attracted the popular moniker of 'Wowser' from an unsympathetic press, he regarded his moral advocacy as intimately linked to his mercy ministries. He enjoyed a personal affinity with the poor of his parish and was all too aware of the untold harm that family breakdown, sexual immorality, gambling and alcohol abuse could visit upon society's most vulnerable. For his decades of service to parish ministry and the Hammond Pioneer Homes, the 'fighting cleric' was recognised with an Order of Australia Medal (OAM) in 1993.[27] In the context of the later twentieth-century, Judd had represented one of the great standard-bearers for the Evangelical tradition of social activism in Australia.

7.3. Conclusion

Always taking the local parish as its starting point, this activist Evangelical tradition was nourished considerably by Simeon in Britain and nurtured here in Australia by the lives of Boyce, Hammond, Judd and many others. Far from representing a worldly 'social gospel' substitute to the saving gospel of Jesus Christ, this longstanding practice of charitable outreach served as an adornment to the gospel of personal salvation in Christ. In essence, it represented the practical outworking of the believer's spiritual rebirth and new life in Jesus. In the spirit of Wilberforce's 'practical Christianity', Simeon and his Australian disciples studiously avoided the tendency of much of Evangelicalism to divorce evangelism from social action. In so doing, their expression of faith maintained the equilibrium of conversionism, biblicism, crucicentrism and activism necessary for the optimal flourishing of Evangelical Christianity.

---

[25] Bernard Judd, *Sunsets to Sunrises: Commemorating the 60th Anniversary of the Beginning of Hammondville*, (Hammondville Homes for Senior Citizens, Sydney), p 2, cited in Lake, *Faith in Action*, p 140.

[26] Lance Shilton, *Speaking Out: A Life of Urban Ministry: The Autobiography of Lance Shilton* (Sydney: Centre for the Study of Australian Christianity, 1997).

[27] Alan Gill, 'Fighting Cleric's Service Honoured', *The Sydney Morning Herald*, 14 June 1993, p 9.

8. Bibliography

8.1. Primary Sources

Boyce, Francis Bertie, *Fourscore Years and Seven: Memoirs of Archdeacon Boyce, for over Sixty Years a Clergyman of the Church of England in New South Wales* (Sydney: Angus and Robertson, 1934)

Brown, Abner, *Recollections of the Conversation Parties of the Revd Charles Simeon* (London: Hamilton, Adams, & Co., 1863)

Carus, William, *Memoirs of the Life of the Revd Charles Simeon*, 3rd edn (London: Hatchard and Son, 1847)

Guinness, Howard, 'Australia', in *Christ and the Colleges: A History of the Inter-Vasity Fellowship of Evangelical Unions* (London: IVF, 1934), pp 169-88

Jones, Charles Alfred, *A History of the Jesus Lane Sunday School, Cambridge; With Short Biographical Notices of Some Deceased Teachers, and Lists of Superintendents, Teachers Etc. From Its Commencement* (London: William Macintosh, 1864)

Newton, John, *Memoirs of the Life of the Late Revd William Grimshaw* (London: Baynes and Son, 1825)

Peacock, George, *Observations on the Statutes of the University of Cambridge* (London, 1841)

Simeon, Charles, *Horae Homileticae or Discourses (in the Form of Skeletons) upon the Whole Scriptures* (London: Richard Watts, 1819), I

——, *Horae Homileticae or Discourses (in the Form of Skeletons) upon the Whole Scriptures* (London: Richard Watts, 1819), III

——, *Horae Homileticae or Discourses (in the Form of Skeletons) upon the Whole Scriptures* (London: Richard Watts, 1819), XVI

——, *Horae Homileticae or Discourses (in the Form of Skeletons) upon the Whole Scriptures* (London: Richard Watts, 1819), XVII

——, *Horae Homileticae or Discourses (in the Form of Skeletons) upon the Whole Scriptures* (London: Richard Watts, 1819), XVIII

Sidney, Edwin, *The Life of the Revd Rowland Hill* (London: Baldwin & Cradock, 1834)

'St Matthias, Draft Parish Profile', 2003, Hodkinson: 20.123

Sumner, John Bird, *A Charge Delivered to the Clergy of the Diocese of Chester at the Primary Visitation in August and September 1829* (London: Hatchard and Son, 1829)

Wesley, John, *The Works of Revd John Wesley* (New York: J & J Harper, 1826), I

——, *The Works of the Revd John Wesley*, ed. by Joseph Benson (Thomas Blanchard, 1809), IV

8.2. Secondary Sources

Anderson, D.G., 'The Bishop's Society, 1856-1958: A History of the Sydney Anglican Home Mission Society' (unpublished Ph.D. Thesis, University of Wollongong, 1990)

Angell, Stephen Ward, and Pink Dandelion, eds., *The Oxford Handbook of Quaker Studies*, Oxford Handbooks, 1st ed (Oxford: Oxford University, 2013)

Angus, David, ed., *Decisive Years: Experiences of Christian University Students* (Melbourne, 2005)

Atherstone, Andrew, 'Evangelical Mission and Anglican Church Order: Charles Simeon Reconsidered', in *Preachers, Pastors, and Ambassadors: Puritan Wisdom for Today's Church : St. Antholin Lectures 2001-2010*, ed. Lee Gatiss (London: Latimer Trust, 2011)

Balleine, George, *A History of the Evangelical Party in the Church of England* (London: Church Book Room, 1951)

Bebbington, David, *Evangelicalism in Modern Britain: A History from the 1730s to the 1980s* (London: Unwin Hyman, 1989)

Bennett, John, 'Charles Simeon and the Evangelical Missionary Movement. A Study of Voluntarism and Church Mission Tensions' (unpublished Ph.D. Thesis, Edinburgh, 1992)

———, 'The Legacy of Charles Simeon', *International Bulletin of Missionary Research* <https://www.questia.com/magazine/1G1-15435589/the-legacy-of-charles-simeon>

Bonwick, James, *Australia's First Preacher: The Revd Richard Johnson, First Chaplain of New South Wales* (London: Sampson Low, Marston & Co., 1898)

Bradbury, John L., *Chester College and the Training of Teachers, 1839-1975* (Chester: Governors of Chester College, 1975)

Braga, Stuart, *A Century Preaching Christ: Katoomba Christian Convention, 1903-2003* (Sydney: KCC, 2003)

Braga, Stuart, and Patricia Braga, *All His Benefits: Young and Deck Families* (Self Published, 2013)

Braithwaite, Joseph Brevan, *Memoirs of Joseph John Gurney with Selection from His Journal and Correspondence* (Norwich: Fletcher and Alexander, 1854)

Brown, Ford, *Fathers of the Victorians: The Age of Wilberforce* (Cambridge: Cambridge University Press, 1961)

Cable, Kenneth, 'Johnson, Richard (1753-1827)', in *Australian Dictionary of Biography*, National Centre of Biography, online edition (Australian National University, 1967) <http://adb.anu.edu.au/biography/johnson-richard-2275/text2921>

Cable, Kenneth J., 'Francis Bertie Boyce (1844-1931)', in *Australian Dictionary of Biography* (Melbourne: Melbourne University Press, 1979)

Calvin, John, *Institutes of the Christian Religion: In Two Volumes*, ed. John Thomas MacNeill, trans. Ford Lewis Battles (London: Westminster John Knox, 1960)

Coggan, Donald, ed., *Christ and the Colleges: A History of the Inter-Varsity Fellowship of Evangelical Unions* (London: IVF, 1934)

———, *These Were His Gifts* (Exeter: University of Exeter, 1974)

Cowie, Leonard W., 'Simeon, Charles (1759-1836)', in *Oxford Dictionary of National Biography*, online edition, Oct 2005 (OUP, 2004) <http://www.oxforddnb.com.rp.nla.gov.au/view/article/25559>

———, 'Venn, Henry (1725-1797)', in *Oxford Dictionary of National Biography*, online edition, May 2010 (OUP, 2004) <http://www.oxforddnb.com.rp.nla.gov.au/view/article/28184>

Cowper, William Macquarie, *Episcopate of Frederic Barker, Bishop of Sydney and Metropolitan of Australia: A Memoir* (London: Hatchards, 1888)

Cunich, Peter, David Hoyle, Eamon Duffy, and Ronald Hyam, *A History of Magdalene College, 1428-1988* (Cambridge: Magdalene College Publications, 1994)

Davis, P.D., 'Bishop Barker and Education' (unpublished M.Ed Thesis, University of Sydney, 1963)

Dudley-Smith, Timothy, *John Stott: The Making of a Leader* (Leicester: IVP, 1999)

Fielder, Geraint, *Lord of the Years: Sixty Years of Student Witness* (Leicester: IVP, 1988)

Gascoigne, John, *Cambridge in the Age of the Enlightenment: Science, Religion and Politics from the Restoration to the French Revolution* (Cambridge: CUP, 1988)

Gatiss, Lee, *Strangely Warmed: Whitfield, Toplady, Simeon and Wesley's Arminian Campaigns* (London: Latimer, 2014)

Gill, Alan, 'Fighting Cleric's Service Honoured', *The Sydney Morning Herald*, 14 June 1993, p 9

Gladwin, Michael, 'Marsden's Generals: Metropolitan Roots of Marsden's Mission', in *Launching Marsden's Mission. The Beginnings of the Church Missionary Society in New Zealand, Viewed from New South Wales*, ed. Peter Bolt and David Pettett (Latimer Trust, 2014)

Gouldstone, Timothy, *The Rise and Decline of Anglican Idealism in the Nineteenth Century* (Palgrave MacMillan, 2005)

Green, Vivian, *Religion at Oxford and Cambridge* (London: SCM, 1964)

Harrison, John F.C., 'Methodism', in *The Oxford Companion to British History*, ed. John Cannon and Robert Crowcroft, 2nd edn (Oxford: OUP, 2015)

Heiser, F.B., *The Story of Saint Aiden's College Birkenhead, 1847-1947* (Chester: Phillipson & Goulder, 1950)

Hindmarsh, D. Bruce, 'Milner, Joseph (1745-1797)', in *Oxford Dictionary of National Biography*, online edition, May 2010 (OUP, 2004) <http://www.oxforddnb.com.rp.nla.gov.au/view/article/18792>

Hofstetter, Michael, *The Romantic Idea of a University: England and Germany, 1770-1850* (Basingstoke: Palgrave, 2001)

Hopkins, Hugh Evans, *Charles Simeon of Cambridge* (Eugene, Oregon: Wipf & Stock, 1977)

Hylson-Smith, Kenneth, *Evangelicals in the Church of England: 1734-1984* (Edinburgh: T & T Clark, 1988)

Johnson, Douglas, *Contending for the Faith: A History of the Evangelical Movement in Universities and Colleges* (Leicester: IVP, 1979)

Karskens, Grace, *The Colony: A History of Early Sydney* (Sydney: Allen & Unwin, 2009)

Kings, Graham, 'Judicious or Precipitate? Evangelicals and Order in the Church of England', *Fulcrum Newsletter*, December 2005

Knox, Keven C., 'Milner, Isaac (1750-1820)', in *Oxford Dictionary of National Biography*, online edition, May 2010 (OUP, 2004) <http://www.oxforddnb.com.rp.nla.gov.au/view/article/18788>

Lake, Meredith, *Faith in Action: Hammondcare* (Sydney: UNSW Press, 2013)

——, 'Hammond, Robert Brodribb Stewart', in *Dictionary of Sydney*, 2012 <http://dictionaryofsydney.org/entry/hammond_robert_brodribb_stewart>

——, *Proclaiming Jesus Christ as Lord: A History of the Sydney University Evangelical Union* (EU Graduates Fund, 2005)

Loane, Marcus L., *A Centenary History of Moore Theological College* (Sydney: Angus and Robertson, 1955)

Lowman, Pete, *The Day of His Power: A History of the International Fellowship of Evangelical Students* (Leicester: IVP, 1983)

Maple, Grant S., 'Evangelical Anglicanism – Dominant, Defensive or in Decline? A Study of Church Life and Organisation in the Diocese of Sydney during the Episcopate of Frederic Barker, 1855-1882' (unpublished M.A. Hons. Thesis, Macquarie University, 1992)

Marsden, J.B., *Memoirs of the Life and Labours of the Revd Samuel Marsden, of Parramatta, Senior Chaplain of New South Wales: And of His Early Connexion with the Missions to New Zealand and Tahiti* (London: Religious Tract Society, 1858)

McConnell, Anita, 'Farish, William (1759-1837)', in *Oxford Dictionary of National Biography*, online edition, May 2010 (OUP, 2004)

Milner, Joseph, *Practical Sermons* (London: Cadell & Davies, 1821)

Moule, Handley Carr Glyn, *Charles Simeon* (London: Methuen & Co., 1892)

Munden, Alan, 'Charles Simeon, 1759-1836', in *The Heart of Faith: Following Christ in the Church of England*, ed. Andrew Atherstone (Cambridge: Lutterworth, 2008)

Piggin, Stuart, *Spirit of a Nation: The Story of Australia's Christian Heritage* (Sydney: Strand Publishing, 2004)

Pollard, Arthur, 'The Influence and Significance of Simeon's Work', in *Charles Simeon (1759-1836): Essays Written in Commemoration of His Bi-Centenary by Members of the Evangelical Fellowship for Theological Literature* (London: SPCK, 1959)

Pollock, John, *A Cambridge Movement* (London: John Murray, 1953)

Prime, Dereck, *Charles Simeon: An Ordinary Pastor of Extraordinary Influence, History Today* (Leominster: Day One, 2011)

Prince, John, and Moyra Prince, *Out of the Tower* (Sydney: ANZEA Publishers, 1987)

Pullen, Robert A., and Kenneth J. Burnley, *Set Upon a Hill: The Story of St. Mary's Church and Parish Upton, Wirral* (Upton: St Mary's Parish Church, 1993)

Rack, Henry D., 'Holy Club (act. 1729-c.1738)', in *Oxford Dictionary of National Biography*, online edition, May 2012 (OUP, 2004) <http://www.oxforddnb.com.rp.nla.gov.au/view/theme/96375>

——, 'Wesley, John (1703-1791)', in *Oxford Dictionary of National Biography*, online edition, May 2010 (OUP, 2004) <http://www.oxforddnb.com.rp.nla.gov.au/view/article/29069>

Robin, Arthur de Quetteville, *Charles Perry, Bishop of Melbourne: The Challenges of a Colonial Episcopate, 1847-76* (Nedlands: University of Western Australia Press, 1967)

Scotland, Nigel, *The Life and Work of John Bird Sumner, Evangelical Archbishop* (Leominster: Gracewing, 1995)

Searby, Peter, *A History of the University of Cambridge: Volume 3, 1750-1870* (Cambridge: Cambridge University Press, 1997)

Shilton, Lance, *Speaking Out: A Life of Urban Ministry: The Autobiography of Lance Shilton* (Sydney: Centre for the Study of Australian Christianity, 1997)

Smyth, Charles, *Simeon and Church Order: A Study in the Evangelical Revival in Cambridge in the Eighteenth Century* (London: Cambridge, 1940)

Steer, Roger, *Church on Fire: The Story of Anglican Evangelicals* (London: Hodder & Stoughton, 1998)

Stephen, James, *Essays in Ecclesiastical Biography*, 4th edn (London: Longman, Green, Longman and Roberts, 1860)

Stott, John, 'Charles Simeon' (unpublished address, Taylor University, Upland, Indiana, U.S.A., 2004) <https://vimeo.com/17650814>

Thompson, David M., *Cambridge Theology in the Nineteenth Century: Enquiry, Controversy and Truth* (Aldershot: Ashgate, 2008)

Trevelyan, George M., *English Social History: A Survey of Six Centuries, Chaucer to Queen Victoria* (London: Longmans, 1942)

———, *Life and Letters of Lord Macaulay* (London: Longmans Green, 1881)

Turney, Clifford, Ursula Bygott, and Peter Chippendale, *Australia's First: A History of the University of Sydney Volume 1, 1850-1939* (Sydney: Hale & Iremonger, 1991)

Venn, Henry, *The Life and a Selection from the Letters of the Late Revd Henry Venn*, ed. John Venn, 6th edn (London, 1855)

Venn, John, *Annals of a Clerical Family: Being Some Account of the Family and Descendants of William Venn, Vicar of Otterton, Devon, 1600-1621* (Cambridge: CUP, 1904)

Walsh, J.D., 'The Magdalene Evangelicals', *Church Quarterly Review*, 159 (1958)

Wannan, Bill, *Very Strange Tales: The Turbulent Times of Samuel Marsden* (Melbourne: Lansdowne, 1962)

Warren, Max, *Charles Simeon* (London: Church Book Room, 1959)

Wolffe, John, *The Expansion of Evangelicalism: The Age of Wilberforce, More, Chalmers and Finney* (Nottingham: IVP, 2006)

Yarwood, A.T., 'Marsden, Samuel (1765-1838)', in *Australian Dictionary of Biography*, National Centre of Biography, online edition (Australian National University, 1967) <http://adb.anu.edu.au/biography/marsden-samuel-2433/text3237>

———, *Samuel Marsden: The Great Survivor* (Carlton, Vic.: Melbourne University Press, 1977)

———, 'The Making of a Colonial Chaplain: Samuel Marsden and the Elland Society, 1765-93', *Australian Historical Studies*, 16 (1975), 362–80

———, 'The Missionary Marsden: An Australian View', *New Zealand Journal of History*, 4 (1970)

If you have enjoyed this book, you might like to consider
- *supporting the work of the Latimer Trust*
- *reading more of our publications*
- *recommending them to others*

See www.latimertrust.org for more information.

Latimer Publications

Latimer Studies

LS 01	The Evangelical Anglican Identity Problem	Jim Packer
LS 02	The ASB Rite A Communion: A Way Forward	Roger Beckwith
LS 03	The Doctrine of Justification in the Church of England	Robin Leaver
LS 04	Justification Today: The Roman Catholic and Anglican Debate	R. G. England
LS 05/06	Homosexuals in the Christian Fellowship	David Atkinson
LS 07	Nationhood: A Christian Perspective	O. R. Johnston
LS 08	Evangelical Anglican Identity: Problems and Prospects	Tom Wright
LS 09	Confessing the Faith in the Church of England Today	Roger Beckwith
LS 10	A Kind of Noah's Ark? The Anglican Commitment to Comprehensiveness	Jim Packer
LS 11	Sickness and Healing in the Church	Donald Allister
LS 12	Rome and Reformation Today: How Luther Speaks to the New Situation	James Atkinson
LS 13	Music as Preaching: Bach, Passions and Music in Worship	Robin Leaver
LS 14	Jesus Through Other Eyes: Christology in a Multi-faith Context	Christopher Lamb
LS 15	Church and State Under God	James Atkinson,
LS 16	Language and Liturgy	Gerald Bray, Steve Wilcockson, Robin Leaver
LS 17	Christianity and Judaism: New Understanding, New Relationship	James Atkinson
LS 18	Sacraments and Ministry in Ecumenical Perspective	Gerald Bray
LS 19	The Functions of a National Church	Max Warren
LS19 (2nd ed.)	British Values and the National Church: Essays on Church and State from 1964-2014	Ed. David Holloway
LS 20/21	The Thirty-Nine Articles: Their Place and Use Today	Jim Packer, Roger Beckwith
LS 22	How We Got Our Prayer Book	T.W. Drury, Roger Beckwith
LS 23/24	Creation or Evolution: a False Antithesis?	Mike Poole, Gordon Wenham
LS 25	Christianity and the Craft	Gerard Moate
LS 26	ARCIC II and Justification	Alister McGrath
LS 27	The Challenge of the Housechurches	Tony Higton, Gilbert Kirby
LS 28	Communion for Children? The Current Debate	A. A. Langdon
LS 29/30	Theological Politics	Nigel Biggar
LS 31	Eucharistic Consecration in the First Four Centuries and its Implications for Liturgical Reform	Nigel Scotland
LS 32	A Christian Theological Language	Gerald Bray
LS 33	Mission in Unity: The Bible and Missionary Structures	Duncan McMann
LS 34	Stewards of Creation: Environmentalism in the Light of Biblical Teaching	Lawrence Osborn
LS 35/36	Mission and Evangelism in Recent Thinking: 1974-1986	Robert Bashford
LS 37	Future Patterns of Episcopacy: Reflections in Retirement	Stuart Blanch
LS 38	Christian Character: Jeremy Taylor and Christian Ethics Today	David Scott
LS 39	Islam: Towards a Christian Assessment	Hugh Goddard
LS 40	Liberal Catholicism: Charles Gore and the Question of Authority	G. F. Grimes
LS 41/42	The Christian Message in a Multi-faith Society	Colin Chapman
LS 43	The Way of Holiness 1: Principles	D. A. Ousley
LS 44/45	The Lambeth Articles	V. C. Miller

LS 46	*The Way of Holiness 2: Issues*	D. A. Ousley
LS 47	*Building Multi-Racial Churches*	John Root
LS 48	*Episcopal Oversight: A Case for Reform*	David Holloway
LS 49	*Euthanasia: A Christian Evaluation*	Henk Jochemsen
LS 50/51	*The Rough Places Plain: AEA 1995*	
LS 52	*A Critique of Spirituality*	John Pearce
LS 53/54	*The Toronto Blessing*	Martyn Percy
LS 55	*The Theology of Rowan Williams*	Garry Williams
LS 56/57	*Reforming Forwards? The Process of Reception and the Consecration of Woman as Bishops*	Peter Toon
LS 58	*The Oath of Canonical Obedience*	Gerald Bray
LS 59	*The Parish System: The Same Yesterday, Today And For Ever?*	Mark Burkill
LS 60	*'I Absolve You': Private Confession and the Church of England*	Andrew Atherstone
LS 61	*The Water and the Wine: A Contribution to the Debate on Children and Holy Communion*	Roger Beckwith, Andrew Daunton-Fear
LS 62	*Must God Punish Sin?*	Ben Cooper
LS 63	*Too Big For Words? The Transcendence of God and Finite Human Speech*	Mark D. Thompson
LS 64	*A Step Too Far: An Evangelical Critique of Christian Mysticism*	Marian Raikes
LS 65	*The New Testament and Slavery: Approaches and Implications*	Mark Meynell
LS 66	*The Tragedy of 1662: The Ejection and Persecution of the Puritans*	Lee Gatiss
LS 67	*Heresy, Schism & Apostasy*	Gerald Bray
LS 68	*Paul in 3D: Preaching Paul as Pastor, Story-teller and Sage*	Ben Cooper
LS69	*Christianity and the Tolerance of Liberalism: J.Gresham Machen and the Presbyterian Controversy of 1922-1937*	Lee Gatiss
LS70	*An Anglican Evangelical Identity Crisis: The Churchman–Anvil Affair of 1981-4*	Andrew Atherstone
LS71	*Empty and Evil: The worship of other faiths in 1 Corinthians 8-10 and today*	Rohintan Mody
LS72	*To Plough or to Preach: Mission Strategies in New Zealand during the 1820s*	Malcolm Falloon
LS73	*Plastic People: How Queer Theory is changing us*	Peter Sanlon
LS74	*Deification and Union with Christ: Salvation in Orthodox and Reformed thought*	Slavko Eždenci
LS75	*As It Is Written: Interpreting the Bible with Boldness*	Benjamin Sargent
LS76	*Light From Dark Ages? An Evangelical Critique of Celtic Spirituality*	Marian Raikes
LS77	*The Ethics of Usury*	Ben Cooper
LS78	*For Us and For Our Salvation: 'Limited Atonement' in the Bible, Doctrine, History and Ministry*	Lee Gatiss
LS79	*Positive Complementarianism: The Key Biblical Texts*	Ben Cooper
LS80	*Were they Preaching 'Another Gospel'? Justification by faith in the Second Century*	Andrew Daunton-Fear
LS81	*Thinking Aloud: Responding to the Contemporary Debate about Marriage, Sexuality and Reconciliation*	Martin Davie
LS82	*Spells, Sorcerers and Spirits: Magic and the Occult in the Bible*	Kirsten Birkett

Latimer Briefings

LB01	The Church of England: What it is, and what it stands for	R. T. Beckwith
LB02	Praying with Understanding: Explanations of Words and Passages in the Book of Common Prayer	R. T. Beckwith
LB03	The Failure of the Church of England? The Church, the Nation and the Anglican Communion	A. Pollard
LB04	Towards a Heritage Renewed	H.R.M. Craig
LB05	Christ's Gospel to the Nations: The Heart & Mind of Evangelicalism Past, Present & Future	Peter Jensen
LB06	Passion for the Gospel: Hugh Latimer (1485–1555) Then and Now. A commemorative lecture to mark the 450th anniversary of his martyrdom in Oxford	A. McGrath
LB07	Truth and Unity in Christian Fellowship	Michael Nazir-Ali
LB08	Unworthy Ministers: Donatism and Discipline Today	Mark Burkill
LB09	Witnessing to Western Muslims: A Worldview Approach to Sharing Faith	Richard Shumack
LB10	Scarf or Stole at Ordination? A Plea for the Evangelical Conscience	Andrew Atherstone
LB11	How to Write a Theology Essay	Michael P. Jensen
LB12	Preaching: A Guidebook for Beginners	Allan Chapple
LB13	Justification by Faith: Orientating the Church's teaching and practice to Christ (Toon Lecture 1)	Michael Nazir-Ali
LB14	"Remember Your Leaders": Principles and Priorities for Leaders from Hebrews 13	Wallace Benn
LB15	How the Anglican Communion came to be and where it is going	Michael Nazir-Ali
LB16	Divine Allurement: Cranmer's Comfortable Words	Ashley Null
LB17	True Devotion: In Search of Authentic Spirituality	Allan Chapple
LB18	Commemorating War and Praying for Peace: A Christian reflection on the Armed Forces	John Neal

Anglican Foundations Series

FWC	The Faith We Confess: An Exposition of the 39 Articles	Gerald Bray
AF02	The 'Very Pure Word of God': The Book of Common Prayer as a Model of Biblical Liturgy	Peter Adam
AF03	Dearly Beloved: Building God's People Through Morning and Evening Prayer	Mark Burkill
AF04	Day by Day: The Rhythm of the Bible in the Book of Common Prayer	Benjamin Sargent
AF05	The Supper: Cranmer and Communion	Nigel Scotland
AF06	A Fruitful Exhortation: A Guide to the Homilies	Gerald Bray
AF07	Instruction in the Way of the Lord: A Guide to the Prayer Book Catechism	Martin Davie
AF08	Till Death Us Do Part: "The Solemnization of Matrimony" in the Book of Common Prayer	Simon Vibert
AF09	'Sure and Certain Hope': Death and Burial in the Book of Common Prayer	Andrew Cinnamond

Latimer Books

GGC	*God, Gays and the Church: Human Sexuality and Experience in Christian Thinking*	eds. Lisa Nolland, Chris Sugden, Sarah Finch
WTL	*The Way, the Truth and the Life: Theological Resources for a Pilgrimage to a Global Anglican Future*	eds. Vinay Samuel, Chris Sugden, Sarah Finch
AEID	*Anglican Evangelical Identity – Yesterday and Today*	J.I.Packer, N.T.Wright
IB	*The Anglican Evangelical Doctrine of Infant Baptism*	John Stott, Alec Motyer
BF	*Being Faithful: The Shape of Historic Anglicanism Today*	Theological Resource Group of GAFCON
TPG	*The True Profession of the Gospel: Augustus Toplady and Reclaiming our Reformed Foundations*	Lee Gatiss
SG	*Shadow Gospel: Rowan Williams and the Anglican Communion Crisis*	Charles Raven
TTB	*Translating the Bible: From William Tyndale to King James*	Gerald Bray
PWS	*Pilgrims, Warriors, and Servants: Puritan Wisdom for Today's Church*	ed. Lee Gatiss
PPA	*Preachers, Pastors, and Ambassadors: Puritan Wisdom for Today's Church*	ed. Lee Gatiss
CWP	*The Church, Women Bishops and Provision: The Integrity of Orthodox Objections to the Proposed Legislation Allowing Women Bishops*	
TSF	*The Truth Shall Set You Free: Global Anglicans in the 21ˢᵗ Century*	ed. Charles Raven
LMM	*Launching Marsden's Mission: The Beginnings of the Church Missionary Society in New Zealand, viewed from New South Wales*	eds. Peter G Bolt David B. Pettett
MST1	*Listen To Him: Reading and Preaching Emmanuel in Matthew*	Ed. Peter Bolt
GWC	*The Genius of George Whitefield: Reflections on his Ministry from 21ˢᵗ Century Africa*	Ed. Benjamin Dean & Adriaan Neele

www.ingramcontent.com/pod-product-compliance
Lightning Source LLC
Chambersburg PA
CBHW031629040426

42452CB00007B/738